P9-DNM-321

A DIFFERENT KIND OF MIRACLE

EMILIE BARNES

HARVEST HOUSE™ PUBLISHERS

EUGENE, OREGON

A DIFFERENT KIND OF MIRACLE
Copyright © 2002 by Harvest House Publishers
Eugene, Oregon 97402

Library of Congress Cataloging-in-Publication Data
Barnes, Emilie.
    A different kind of miracle / Emilie Barnes with Anne Christian Buchanan.
        p. cm.
    Includes bibliographical references.
    ISBN 0-7369-0904-4 (alk. paper)
    1. Cancer—Patients—Religious life. 2. Consolation. I. Buchanan,
    Anne Christian. II. Title.
    BV4910.33 .B36 2002
    248.8'6196994—dc21   2002004278

02 03 04 05 06 07 08 09 10 11 / RDC-MS / 10 9 8 7 6 5 4 3 2 1

TO MY DEAR ONES:

Brad, my "soul son." You cheered me on with "You can do it, Mom." And I did.

Jenny, my precious one. Our deepening relationship has been one of the Lord's great gifts in my illness.

Bill, our new "son-in-love." You chose to embrace a family as well as a wife.

Christine, Chad, Bevan, Bradley Joe, and Weston, my wonderful grandchildren. Thank you for your prayers, your beautiful smiles, your cute notes and pictures, and especially the warm hugs that gave me strength. You are a big part of your Grammy's healing.

And, of course, my Bob—my sweetheart, my partner, and my hero. I know so much more about God because of the ways you show love to me.

To old friends and new friends, friends close by and far away. You brought me strawberries and rubbed my feet and wept with me and even cleaned up after me. Best of all, you carried me with your prayers. Without your love and support, I would never have made it.

To the doctors, nurses, and staff of Hoag Cancer Clinic in Newport Beach, California, and the Fred Hutchinson Cancer Research Center in Seattle, Washington. You thought you were just doing your job, but I see you for what you are—living instruments of God's grace and healing.

And finally to Dan Rapoi, my bone marrow donor and my brother in Christ. You didn't pass up the opportunity to save a life. Not to be corny, I thank you from the very marrow of my being— and so do my family and friends. In a sense, you'll be a part of everything the Lord accomplishes through me in the future.

CONTENTS

Prologue
The Gift I Didn't Want to Open   9

1. Songs in a Foreign Land
*Where was God when my life fell apart—
and then got worse?*   17

2. The Cupboard's Not Bare
*What I found in my life to carry
me through*   45

3. Leaning in the Long Hours
Reluctant lessons of waiting and pain   65

4. Lord of the Locust Years
What I gained when I lost so much   83

5. Living in His Presence
*Fifteen minutes with God...and how
they grew*   109

6. Cloudy, with Patches of Sun
*Finding comfort and joy in
times of sorrow*   131

7. Hand in Heart in Hand
*The healing ministry of
loving relationships*   149

8. What I Know That I Know
*Reflections on healing, death,
and what comes next*   175

Epilogue
Every Day Is Christmas   197

Notes   201

The Gift I Didn't Want to Open

Every good and perfect gift is from above, coming down from the Father of the heavenly lights, who does not change like shifting shadows. He chose to give us birth through the word of truth, that we might be a kind of firstfruits of all he created.

—JAMES 1:17-18

THE GIFT I DIDN'T WANT TO OPEN

_⌒_

Have you ever received a gift that just didn't feel like a gift at the time?

That happened to me several years ago, when the large, beautifully wrapped package arrived for me from Bailey Smith Ministries in Georgia.

I was pretty sure it contained some sort of gracious offering sent in response to my illness. The women's conference put on by Bailey Smith Ministries was one of the first I had to cancel when my cancer was diagnosed.

Now, as I stared at the package on the table, a lot of conflicting feelings ran through me.

I felt awful about not keeping my commitment to speak.

I felt touched that the Bailey Smith people would care enough to send me a present even after I let them down.

I felt all but overcome by the discomfort and fatigue that filled my days back then.

But what I felt most of all as I looked at that elegant box was dread.

I'm not proud of this, but all I could think of as I stared at that box was *If I open it, I'm going to have to write a thank-you note!*

You may laugh. But I've always felt it is so important to respond promptly and graciously to gifts. And in this case I didn't think I could summon the energy to do it. So I did the strong, mature thing. I left the box sitting there on the table!

It took me literally weeks to open that package. Every day it sat there—first on the table and then on a bench, reminding me how weak I was, how sick I was, how even activities that used to be a joy were now a burden for me.

Finally, with my husband Bob's encouragement, I steeled myself to open that present I didn't want to open. I pulled on the ribbon, removed the wrapping, lifted the lid.

And then…what a blessing! Inside that box were hundreds and hundreds of envelopes, each with my name on it—*spelled correctly!* And inside the envelopes were hundreds and hundreds of loving, gracious cards.

I learned later that when I was forced to cancel, the conference staff called DaySpring Cards, who agreed to donate twelve hundred get-well cards. And then the staff asked every single woman at the conference to write me a card.

Can you believe it? There were twelve hundred cards in that box—and oh, the loveliness they contained. Most of the women wrote notes of comfort, compassion, and cheer. Many shared stories of their own trials and Scriptures that had been meaningful to them in their difficulties.

What encouragement those cards brought me as I began to read through them! What a beautiful gift they were to me—not just at the moment, but throughout the course of my illness. I would read and reread them during my long hours at home and draw strength and comfort from the love that shone through those letters. I still have them all—gathered in a collection of baskets in my bedroom office.

But looking back, I can still recall how reluctant I was to open that gift. I can still picture it there on the table, mocking me, daring me to open it. All I could see was the difficulty it represented for me, when really it was full of hope and comfort and encouragement.

I think we often feel that way about what the Lord sends into our lives—the gifts of our days, of our circumstances, of the things that happen to us. They come to us all wrapped up in mystery. And unlike the Bailey Smith package, they're not all wrapped beautifully. Some look ugly and forbidding and terrifying. They're not the kind of thing we'd like to have in our lives at all, and we're certainly not eager to open them, even when our faith reminds us that God is in charge.

Needless to say, that's the way I felt about the gift that arrived on my doorstep a few years back in the form of a cancer diagnosis. I had been a Christian many, many years. I had ministered to countless women, sharing God's message of hope and healing. I had already unwrapped a number of frightening packages that turned out to contain gifts from the Lord, and I knew he was already at work in this frightening circumstance. I *knew* all would be well.

But still—cancer? Who really wants to open that kind of package when it comes?

Well, today I can state with full confidence that those days of my life that came wrapped in illness, weakness, pain, and fear also contained gifts of comfort and love and courage. They contained joys little and large, as well as the more sober but precious lessons that come from suffering. Best of all, every one of those fearful cancer-wrapped days turned out to be full of God—permeated by his presence. And ultimately, they contained the miracle of healing.

But I have to be honest with you. The miracle I discovered as I unwrapped day after difficult day wasn't exactly the kind I expected.

Not that I really expected cancer healing in 15 minutes a day!

But I never thought God's work would take quite so long, would hurt so much, would take me so many new and unexpected directions.

I thought it would be over quickly. I had a lot to learn about God's timing and God's purposes.

I thought I'd take it all in stride and just go on with my life and ministry. I had no idea how profoundly and permanently everything would change.

I expected to be healed spontaneously through prayer and the laying on of hands, helped along by natural health practices. But while prayer was indeed crucial and my healthy lifestyle might have helped, God accomplished this particular miracle slowly, gradually, and through the knowledge and talents of gifted medical professionals and the loving sacrifice of a brave Canadian disc jockey.

Today, I stand in awe of the miracle of healing I have experienced. It's a different kind of miracle than the ones we often expect—but it's really not so different from the miracles God works every day in the lives of so many.

I've come to believe, in fact, that most of us need to have our ideas about miracles stretched. The reality is that God is mysterious. God is sovereign. And that means that God rarely works the way we think he will.

But God is also faithful. He keeps his promises—and his Word is full of promises for healing. He loves us and longs to give us not only what we need, but so much more. More than anything, he longs to make us his—and he will use any circumstance as a tool to draw us closer, make us part of his redeeming work on this earth. The gift he most passionately wants to give us is the gift of himself.

That, in essence, is what I want to show in this book. By sharing with you the gifts the Lord has given me, the miracles that have unfolded as I unwrapped my painful and fearsome days, I hope I can help you see the miracles God is working in your life even now, the gifts he wants to give you in all the circumstances of all your days.

And even as I write this, I'm aware that your circumstances may be more painful and difficult than mine. Perhaps you're struggling with the aftermath of a divorce or financial disaster. Perhaps you've been dragged down by depression or hindered by multiple sclerosis or arthritis. Perhaps you, too, have been touched by cancer—or have been handed a wearying, frustrating caretaker's role for a loved one who is ill or incapacitated.

It may also be that the specific outcome of your trouble will be different from mine. God willing, you will find healing and restoration on this side of paradise...but it's also possible you'll have to wait until death for the fulfillment of your faith and release from your pain. (Chances are, like me, you'll experience a little of both.) And yet I believe you'll find, as I have found again and again, that God's mercy is wider than anything the day might bring. The healing he offers to all of us encompasses so much more than a simple cure.

Whatever the gift life has left on your doorstep, no matter how ugly the package, I invite you to open it in the confidence that God is in it.

He will not leave you desolate.

One way or another, if you open your arms to him, he will use the gift of your days to fold you closer to his heart and make you truly his.

CHAPTER ONE

Songs in a Foreign Land

How can we sing the songs of the LORD while in a foreign land?

—PSALM 137:4

Where can I go from your Spirit? Where can I flee from your presence? If I go up to the heavens, you are there; if I make my bed in the depths, you are there. If I rise on the wings of the dawn, if I settle on the far side of the sea, even there your hand will guide me, your right hand will hold me fast.

—PSALM 139:7-10

1

SONGS IN A
FOREIGN LAND

*Where was God when my life fell apart—
and then got worse?*

⎯⎯

I'm not the first person to call it Cancerland.

Others before me have noticed that undergoing cancer treatment is a little like journeying through a foreign country where everything is different from what you're used to.

The scenery is strange—largely limited to waiting rooms and therapy rooms, sofas and beds, and the narrow path between home and the doctor's office and the emergency room—but there are moments when the vista widens to show you amazing things about God's truth and the human spirit you would otherwise never have glimpsed.

The sounds are different, too—mostly TV blather and elevator music. The smells—well, we won't go into the smells, but the food is terrible. And the language is difficult, full of strange, mouth-filling jargon.

The best thing about Cancerland is that it's full of good people. If you travel there, you'll meet a number of visiting health professionals (most of whom are efficient and compassionate), an assortment of fellow tourists (many in wigs and turbans, but also helpful and caring), and a number of friends and family members who come along as companions on the journey (the true saints of the land!). Sure, there are a few who are bitter or disillusioned, a few who are thoughtless and rude, but it's still easy to make friends there. There's nothing like a shared journey to make companions out of fellow travelers.

And here's something else I learned while traveling in Cancerland: It's an earthquake zone.

Having grown up in Southern California, I know a little about earthquakes. I've been there for quite a few major shocks and literally hundreds of little ones, so I usually know an earthquake when I feel one. And once I set foot in cancer country, I realized I was also going to be traveling in earthquake country.

One of the first things you learn in earthquake country is that it's not always over when it's over. One shock is often followed by another—sometimes by another and another—and aftershocks can cause as much damage as the initial jolt. So we who live in earthquake zones are taught from an early age that surviving an earthquake is often a matter of hanging on until all the shaking is truly over. And that's certainly what Bob and I have been doing over the past few years as we walk the roads (and corridors) of Cancerland.

Something else we learn in earthquake country is that shocks and aftershocks are a fact of life, that forces are at work beneath the ground we walk on that periodically will shake our foundations. And that's certainly true of cancer country, where so much goes on beneath the surface and there's so little you can control.

How do you live with that kind of reality? You prepare the best you can, making sure your buildings are up to code and your foundations are both strong and flexible. You go about your business, trusting God to carry you through those times when the earth literally shakes. Then...well, then you hold on for dear life and you pray!

And, of course, there's the third thing I learned about both earthquake zones and foreign lands: God lives there, too. This one fact is the heart of my story, which is about the way the Lord sustained me and my family during our journey through the seismic zones of Cancerland.

It has been six years since we first felt the underground rumblings on the road we were traveling—but at first we had no idea we had crossed the border into Cancerland. At that time our lives were busy and full. Our home organization ministry, More Hours in My Day, was successful and growing. Bob and I traveled several weekends a month to speak at conferences around the country, and our books were selling well. Even better, we could see the Lord changing lives and hearts through our ministry.

Our family brought us great joy, with our children, Brad and Jenny, and all five grandchildren living nearby. Our dream home, the converted barn in Riverside, California, where we had lived for more than 30 years, was a peaceful and well-loved retreat. In the spring of 1997, it would even be featured on the cover of *Better Homes and Gardens* magazine!

So much was going well for us in those days. The trouble was, I just didn't *feel* well. I suffered from chronic bronchitis and sinusitis and frequent indigestion, and the constant travel didn't help. Fatigue was a familiar companion. And I was bothered with hard, itchy knots on my body that resembled mosquito bites that refused to be relieved by over-the-counter agents.

On top of that, I was deeply worried about our daughter, Jenny, who had ended her marriage and turned away from the Lord. I ached for her three children, who suffered intensely from the breakup of their home. Bob and I struggled daily with anger toward Jenny for what she had done and worry for her family. (I won't get into Jenny's story here except to say that the miracle of prayer and the persistent love of the Lord were already working miracles in the life of my Jenny. It took a long time, but over the period of four years I saw her change from a frustrated, hurt, rebellious person to a deeply committed woman of God. Her marriage was not restored as I had prayed so many times—but Jenny was transformed. And our relationship was transformed as well as we all learned to wait on the Lord, trust his timing, and obey him in forgiving one another.)

What I see now but couldn't see then was the way God was already working in all of us, building new strength and flexibility into our characters, teaching us to trust and obey and forgive each other, and helping us to thank him in everything, even when the ground all around us was shaking. He was preparing us for what was coming next—which was a series of earthquakes that would shake our foundations even as it renewed our faith in the firm foundation underneath it all.

Even as Jenny's situation began to resolve itself, my health situation just didn't seem to improve. My doctors couldn't figure out what was wrong. Allergy shots and frequent rounds of antibiotics and even sinus surgery failed to help. I had always been a stickler for good nutrition and regular exercise, but healthy foods and vitamin supplements and long daily walks didn't seem to improve matters, either.

I turned to a Christian nutritional specialist in our area, a woman with a Ph.D. in nutrition and a specialization in homeopathic remedies. She decided that my allergy shots and other treatments had poisoned my system and started me on a special diet designed to remove the toxins. To this day I don't know whether this regime actually helped or hurt me. I suspect it helped build my strength for the coming trial even as it prevented me from being diagnosed as quickly as I might have been.

At any rate, although I trusted my "health doctor" and felt my special diet was helping, my family and friends were not so sure. I was losing weight fast. And though my bronchitis went away for a while, it returned with a vengeance, along with chills, vomiting, fever, and recurring abdominal discomfort.

Through all this, I continued to speak, write, travel, and minister. Somehow God gave me the strength to do what he had called me to do. I was often amazed at how he would take over in my weakness to minister to women who needed a touch of his love. But then, when the seminar was over and all the hugs had been given and the books autographed, I would all but collapse. At home I barely managed to get through the days. People began to comment on how thin I looked. I suffered from night sweats and chronic nausea, and a deep cough was always with me.

My family finally insisted that I see another doctor. He took some tests and then referred me to a Christian oncologist, who at last gave me a name for the illness lying behind so many of my symptoms.

He said I was suffering from something called chronic lymphocytic leukemia.

Cancer.

That was truly an earthquake to rival the one that had jolted our family years before with Jenny's divorce. Anyone who has heard that word mentioned in a doctor's office knows what power it has to shake a person's world.

Through my stunned ears, I listened to talk about more tests. I heard the oncologist explain that although this particular form of leukemia moves slowly and I could live with it a long time, I still needed immediate treatment. I heard the dreaded words *chemotherapy* and *radiation,* and I shrank from the idea of injecting my body with chemicals and searing it with radiation.

My health doctor, too, objected vigorously to the proposed treatments. She wasn't sure I had cancer at all, and she asked for two weeks before I made any decisions. I was happy to give her that time, and I solicited the prayers of everybody I knew.

And at the end of those weeks of intense homeopathic treatment, my white cell count was up, other cancer indicators had subsided, and my Christian oncologist was amazed. "I believe in prayer," he said, "and I have no problem with alternative treatments." He suggested I just keep on doing what I was doing, and he saw no reason to proceed with more tests and treatment.

What a relief! What a time of rejoicing! I couldn't wait to build up my strength, to get back to work. All was well. The earthquake was over…until the day two months later when I went to change the sheets on our bed and then doubled over in agony. My entire abdomen seemed to be on fire; I could barely make it to the couch to lie down. By the time Bob and Jenny loaded me into our van and headed for the hospital, I was curled into a fetal position, holding my stomach and moaning.

That night, I underwent emergency surgery for a perforated ulcer the size of a silver dollar. I was in the hospital for more than a week. And Bob had to do something that we had never done during my whole long siege of bronchitis, sinus surgery, or even leukemia.

He canceled seven seminars.

My health doctor assured me this was not a setback. But to me it felt like one—a powerful and painful aftershock. And afterward, though I eventually resumed my speaking schedule and continued with my nutritionist's diet and started walking again and praying for my family, I gradually had to face the fact that I still wasn't getting better. My stomach discomfort, especially, persisted, and nothing the health doctor prescribed seemed to help.

I was rapidly becoming convinced I needed to look elsewhere for medical answers. So we began to ask around. We did some research. And we repeatedly heard the name of an oncologist at the Hoag Hospital Cancer Clinic in Newport Beach, California, about an hour's drive from our home in Riverside. We had lived in Newport Beach years earlier. We had friends there we trusted, and they had nothing but good things to say about Dr. Barth. So we decided to see him for a second opinion. We went through the usual round of tests and then came back to discuss the results with him.

I'll never forget how angry Dr. Barth was on the day he unleashed the next earthquake into our lives. Not angry with us—but angry on our behalf.

"Do you know," he fumed, "that you have a tumor in your abdomen the size of a football?"

No, we didn't know that, but it explained a lot! We weren't in Southern California any more—we had definitely crossed the border into Cancerland.

Dr. Barth told us that instead of suffering from chronic lymphocytic leukemia, I had a rare form of non-Hodgkin's lymphoma called MALT-cell lymphoma, which starts in the lymphatic cells lining organs such as the stomach. It is related to chronic lymphocytic leukemia and produces similar results in the blood—which helps explain the other oncologist's diagnosis. Interestingly enough, this cancer is somehow linked to the presence of a an ulcer-causing bacteria in the stomach called helicobacter pylori—which helps explain my ulcer, though not the fact that the hospital surgeons didn't notice a tumor the size of a football! And early symptoms of MALT-cell lymphoma include allergies, chronic bronchitis, sinusitis, and abdominal discomfort!

The good news was that this cancer, like the leukemia I thought I had, is usually slow-growing, with a good survival rate. On the other hand, my diagnosis had been delayed for so long that immediate treatment was necessary. Because the tumor in my abdomen had wrapped around several organs, surgery was out of the question. I would be treated first with radiation and then with chemotherapy, with the goal of first shrinking the tumor and then removing all traces of the cancer from my bloodstream and lymph system.

It was in the spring of 1998 when Dr. Barth finally diagnosed my lymphoma and prescribed my upcoming series of radiation and chemotherapy—six or seven sessions, each about 21 days apart. At that point Bob called to cancel all our speaking engagements for the rest of the year, assuring those who asked that I looked forward to speaking again the following spring.

About this time we also made the decision to make a temporary move to Newport Beach so we could be closer to the doctor during the three or four months the therapy would take. (Bob would commute back and forth to our home in Riverside to keep the business running, check on the house, and make sure the plants were watered.) We found a townhouse not far from the clinic, moved in enough of our household to feel a little like home—I had to have the armoire full of my teacup collection!—and started the routine that would come to feel so familiar over the next few months.

The actual chemo sessions were more boring than anything else. I would come in and either sit in one of the big recliners or on a cot in the back room of Dr. Barth's office. A member of the clinic's staff—they all came to seem like family to us—would attach a bag of drugs to my "Hickman," a plastic device implanted in my chest to spare me the need for constant IV sticks. I would sit or lie there while the drug was infused into my body. Then Bob would take me home to bed and I would sleep. We would do this for five days in a row, and then we'd take two or three weeks off to see what happened.

What usually happened was that I felt awful right after the therapy and then gradually better until it was time for another weekly session. Chemotherapy is essentially the art of selective poisoning—giving the body just enough toxins to kill the cancer but not the entire person. And though other drugs helped reduce the side effects, I still suffered from frequent nausea and, shall we say, other unpleasant reactions. (Bathrooms make up a lot of the scenery in Cancerland.) Food lost its appeal, and I had to force myself to eat—which was important because Dr. Barth told me every chemo session used at least 3900 calories in my body! Not surprisingly, I was often exhausted after a chemo session and spent most of the time on the couch, resting.

Radiation was also relatively uneventful, although it felt odd to have the therapist write on me with a permanent marker to show the radiation sites and strange to be alone in a room with those big machines manipulated by therapists from outside. For me, the side effects of radiation were similar to that of chemotherapy—constant fatigue, upset stomach, lost appetite. As expected, I lost my hair during the chemotherapy, and my husband, son, and grandsons shaved their heads in solidarity. (We have a picture!) When my hair grew back gray, I decided to leave it that way, and everybody seemed to like my new short silver "do."

The regime of radiation and chemotherapy lasted beyond the three or four months we had allotted. Although most of my body responded well to the regiment, one stubborn type of cell seemed to hold out against treatment. I had more chemo, lost my hair again, and when Christmas rolled around we were still living in Newport Beach.

With the prescribed course of chemo finally finished, I began a round of high-dosage antibiotics. (MALT-cell lymphoma is unusual in that it is associated with a particular kind of bacteria and sometimes responds to such treatments.) Then, in March 1999, we received wonderful news. Dr. Barth pronounced that I was in "HLPR"—high-level partial remission. My tumor had shriveled, and my blood "numbers" were vastly improved. The plan was for us to see him monthly until June, when I would do four weekly treatments of a new treatment, a "monoclonal antibody" called Rituxan that was producing very good results with few side effects in people with similar cancers to mine.

We rejoiced, certain that my healing was on its way and deliverance from my cancer was in sight. I even decided to accept a couple of speaking engagements because I was feeling so much stronger.

Then, in April, another earthquake jarred us. Actually, two tremors, one after another—though we didn't even notice one of them when it first appeared.

The first new quake showed itself with a routine CAT scan. My tumor was growing again. My blood work indicated the cancer was on the move in other parts of my body. To stop it, I would have to go through another series of radiation—20 or 30 treatments over a course of four or five weeks.

This, of course, was acutely disappointing. I dreaded another round of fatigue and the side effects—especially after feeling good for a while. And I didn't want to lose my hair again! But the second thing that happened in April would be the source of even more distress, though it began far more quietly.

I had returned from one of my speaking engagements with an annoying, prickly rash. I treated it with calamine lotion and flew off to my next conference, never guessing that rash was really an attack of shingles.

Shingles, I know now, are basically an adult outbreak of the chickenpox virus—a form of herpes infection that can stay dormant in the body from childhood, then reemerge as a painful rash when the immune system is compromised. If the shingles are not treated immediately, a lingering form of nerve damage called postherpetic neuralgia can wreak havoc in the body for months or even years to come.

This is what happened to me. The initial rash cleared up not long after I contracted it, only to return with a vengeance about three weeks later. The doctor diagnosed the problem and began treatment, but the ongoing pain of the postherpetic neuralgia had already set in. It has persisted through all the years of my cancer treatment and lingers to the present day. Only in the last few months of 2001 did it begin to diminish even slightly.

The pain from this affliction has far surpassed the discomforts of chemo and radiation and any discomfort from the cancer itself. In fact, it was only when my stomach ruptured from the ulcer that I felt any direct pain related to my cancer. But every day for at least three years I experienced the agony of postherpetic neuralgia—stabbing, shooting, burning pains in my torso that made wearing clothes a torture and being touched an ordeal. The degree of the discomfort would change—there were bad days and better ones—but it was always there. Sometimes I could only find a measure of relief by lying absolutely motionless. Although I never reached the point of despair, I could absolutely understand when I read that shingles can lead to intense depression and is a primary cause of suicide among the elderly.

I underwent an intense period of radiation in May 1999. Then we met again with Dr. Barth to review my test results, and the news was not good. The radiation had failed to stop the regrowth of cancer in my body, and more aggressive treatment was needed. Beginning in June, I would have to do two 96-hour sessions of chemotherapy.

I went through the chemo. Again. My hair fell out. Again. The shingles hurt. Still. And after all that we met in Dr. Barth's office to review the results.

The good news was that the actual tumor was almost gone.

The bad news was that the lymphoma was still present in my body and was gaining ground.

It was at this point that Dr. Barth told us I had a 40 to 60 percent chance of survival—"and that's with a miracle."

Well, I had never stopped believing I'd have my miracle. I wasn't about to stop believing now. We still hoped and prayed for a miracle of healing, but now the stakes seemed higher. Now I was truly fighting for my life.

Dr. Barth outlined several courses of treatment we could take. The Rituxan therapy was still a possibility. So was a procedure called a stem cell infusion, in which healthy cells from my blood would be gathered and frozen and then later reinserted to rebuild my bone marrow after very high-dose chemotherapy. And yet another possible treatment would be a bone marrow transplant.

I gasped when I heard that last suggestion. A bone marrow transplant? I had heard that such a procedure was a last resort for only the most desperately ill. And at that point, I couldn't digest the reality that "desperately ill" applied to me.

Rituxan and stem cell infusion seemed like preferable treatments, but it still seemed prudent to check out the possibility of the bone marrow transplant. So we began the long process of finding a donor who would qualify. At that time, six components in the blood had to match to be considered viable. None of my blood relations—Jenny and Brad, my brother—met these criteria. Neither did Bob, his family, or any of our friends. Finally Dr. Barth put out word to the various national and international databases that we were looking for an unrelated donor.

We also canceled the rest of our speaking engagements and began thinking about selling our mail-order business.

Meanwhile, we went on with life the best we could. And life, as usual, was full of ups and downs. (In this way, life in Cancerland is just like life anywhere else.)

The downs, I'm afraid, fell mostly on Bob's shoulders— and in these days I was learning what truly broad shoulders he has. In addition to caring for me—taking me to treatments, supervising my medications, monitoring my condition—he handled all the shopping, cooking, and cleaning. He traveled back and forth to Riverside to take care of our mail-order business, handle our publishing responsibilities, and maintain our home. And he was the primary caregiver for his 85-year-old mother, who had reached the point where she could no longer live alone. As her bodily weakness and mental confusion progressed, we tried keeping her with us at first, but then, as I became sicker, we had to consider a home. Bob moved her to three different facilities, seeking the best option. He visited her four days a week and did her laundry and whatever else he could for her. Our whole family felt the sadness of watching this strong, vital, godly woman decline.

But the joys we experienced during this difficult time were also real and helped us sing even in that foreign land. Ocean views out our balcony window and occasional picnics on the shore reminded me of how much I loved the water and sand. Frequent visits from our children and grandchildren—who loved to be able to visit Papa and Grammy and go to the beach the same day—kept up our spirits. Bob and I built relationships with other patients and their families and grew to love the staff at Dr. Barth's office, and we were able to minister to them as well, giving them books and sharing with them the hope that kept us going.

One of the great gifts of that time was the rekindling of close relationships with a group of friends we had known for years and never really lost touch with. Bob was enjoying the supportive fellowship of a group of like-minded men friends, something he hadn't had in our years of travel. Our new church—actually, a church we had attended years before—gathered round us and ministered to us, even though I was unable to attend regularly. Not long after the earthquake of my "40-to-60 percent" diagnosis, the elders of that church gathered around us, read Scriptures, anointed my forehead with oil, and prayed for my healing.

And always, every single day, I felt the tangible uplift of support from all the people who were praying for me around the country. Some of them were old friends. Some I didn't even know—I found out secondhand that they had put me on their prayer list. Many sent me cards and letters and faxes, shared Scriptures and stories. Through every day, even the most difficult, I leaned on these tangible expressions of God's love for me.

One of the happiest developments of that summer was the acquisition of a new son-in-love. His name is Bill, and he quickly became a source of blessing in our lives. You see, after Jenny rededicated her life to the Lord, she had tried numerous times to reconcile with her former husband, to no avail. Finally, she had decided to move ahead with her life and just concentrate on being a godly mother to her children. And that was when God brought Bill into her life. They met through a friend and gradually, carefully, built a relationship. Eventually it became clear to us as well as to Jenny that this friendly, dependable man was going to be a permanent part of our lives. In the summer of 1999, with my head still bald from the latest round of chemo—but decorated with a pretty scarf and a summery hat—we joyfully celebrated the marriage of our Jenny to Bill. Then, with their brood settled in a beautiful new home an hour away, we looked ahead to the next step, whatever that might be.

The story of the next six months is basically that of trying first one thing, then another, to reverse the progress of cancer in my body. Programs and schedules were devised and then revised all during that fall. I went through one round of stem cell harvesting, but my body just couldn't manufacture enough stem cells to make a stem cell infusion possible. Shortly after New Year's Day I began a course of Rituxan therapy along with other medications, working to build up my system in the event that a qualified bone marrow donor would be found.

In February we received news that two possible donors had been identified, and in April the choice was narrowed down to a single donor—a 23-year-old Canadian—who matched all six of the necessary components in my blood. We weren't allowed to know his name, but we were told he was the only person in any of the databases who was a perfect match for me—and he was willing to give me some of his bone marrow.

Dr. Barth had recommended we have the bone marrow transplant done at the Fred Hutchinson Cancer Research Center, a cutting edge facility in Seattle, Washington. So I continued my treatments while Bob made all the arrangements for us to close up two households—in Newport Beach and in Riverside—and move to Seattle. For at least four months we would live at a Marriott Residence Inn adjacent to the Hutchinson Center—or "the Hutch," as it was commonly called.

Arriving at our Residence Inn "apartment" (basically a hotel suite with a kitchen) was like exploring a new county in Cancerland. For 125 days, our world would basically consist of our two-room suite with kitchenette, the hallways and lobby of the Residence Inn, the waiting rooms and treatment rooms of the Hutch and the University of Washington Hospital, and the shuttle bus that carried us between these places. In these places we would live, eat, and sleep; we would welcome visitors; we would make wonderful new friends and lose some of them to death. In addition to which, of course, I would receive my extreme, last-ditch treatment.

The goal of my bone marrow transplant, as I understand it, was to decimate my immune system with heavy-dosage chemotherapy and radiation, then introduce the donor's bone marrow cells in the hope that they would build me a new, cancer-free immune system. I had to undergo a painful bone marrow biopsy and several days of intense chemotherapy and radiation. But the actual transplant for this amazing procedure seemed surprisingly ordinary—just an IV session with a bag of fluid containing the donor cells. I was given a number of drugs to prevent infection and suppress any immune response to the donor marrow. Then we went back to the Residence Inn to wait for the young Canadian's marrow to take over and build me a new immune system.

The rest of that summer is more or less a blur for me because I was on so much medication. I remember being embarrassed to have anyone see me because graft-versus-host disease, a common reaction to a bone marrow transplant, had turned my skin red and shiny, and the steroid drugs used to fight the graft-versus-host disease had also caused my body to swell and given me pudgy chipmunk cheeks. The shingles pain continued, unresponsive to any treatment we tried. Our front-window view of Lake Union—complete with sailboats—was beautiful and inspiring, but I slept much of the time, and Bob filled his days the best he could.

And during that summer, at a time crucial to my treatment, Bob's mother passed away. My Bob, who loved his mother dearly and had cared for her tenderly for so many years, made the hard choice not to go home for her funeral. He felt I was too sick to be left alone, even for a short time. Instead, we told her goodbye in a small memorial service with a few friends and family members.

After more than a hundred days in Seattle, we were finally given the all-clear to return to Southern California. I was still pink-faced, still puffy, still weak and heavily medicated, still in pain, but my heart rejoiced to be back home...but to a different home.

It was while we were in Seattle, as we came to terms with how long my recovery might take, we had finally decided to make our move to Newport Beach permanent. We loved our Riverside "barn," which housed our offices and store as well as our lives, but the big house and extensive grounds needed more care than we could give it. We also felt the need to remain close to Dr. Barth's office for ongoing treatment. And it just felt right to move ahead into another era of our life.

Working through a real estate agent, we had located a perfect house in a community just blocks from the beach. (The fact that it was available exactly when we needed it, at a price we could afford, was a confirmation to us that the Lord was still at work directing our lives.)

We had made plans to turn over our mail-order business to our friends Sherry and Tim Torelli, who had taken care of our web site and our correspondence for years. Then Brad and Jenny and their families and our Newport Beach friends had worked to paint and remodel our new house and get it ready for us to move into when we came home. (Yet another sign of God's care: Our new son-in-law also happens to be a painting contractor!)

My first task upon returning from Seattle was to sort out our furniture and possessions and decide which ones would be moved into our new smaller digs. This painful task seemed to crystallize all the difficult decisions we had had to make in the past few years, all the losses we had sustained. Our dream house in Riverside was full of memories, full of love, and every item in it seemed to be connected to who we are. I sorted through outfits I had worn at my seminars, furniture that had belonged to my mother, mementos from our travels, souvenirs of my publishing career. How could I choose what to keep?

Strangely, my very illness helped with this task. I was sad to leave the Riverside house behind, but I was also eager for us to have a simpler, less demanding life. The hard process of fighting cancer had somehow made it easier to let go of our old life, which I loved, and to understand that what I loved best—Bob, our family, our witness for the Lord—would still be intact no matter where we lived. So I made decisions about what would go and what would move. Bob stepped in to save some items that in my weariness I wanted to toss. Family members gave some items a home. Many found new homes in an estate sale. And many things, of course, made the move with us—including my teacup collection and our sweet, elderly cat, Mokie, who took to seaside living with true gusto.

By early fall we were settled in our new home with its big, airy living room, its bright pink guest room, its comfy den and clean, convenient kitchen. So much of our furniture and decorations from Riverside fit beautifully in that house—there was even a built-in, glass-door cabinet for my teacups—and there was much that was new as well, including a wealth of beautiful paintings by our friend Zoe Hadley. We loved the neighborhood with its profusion of flowers and friendly neighbors. We also loved the proximity to the beach, my favorite place since childhood.

But what strange days these were for both Bob and me! We had always been active people, accustomed to taking care of our families, running our business, being in control. Now our primary task was to wait for my new bone marrow to take over while keeping track of medications, avoiding infection, and keeping an ear out for aftershocks—rumbling complications that might mean my body was rejecting the new bone marrow.

My job was to rest and build my strength, though the pain from my bout with shingles made recovery difficult. I spent much of my time just lying still, hoping the pain would ease. Bob kept on cooking, cleaning, writing his books, and juggling pills and insurance forms.

My darling Jenny was such a help to us in this time. When we got home from Seattle she told me, "Mom, I'm going to give you a whole year of my time. I'll be available to you whenever you need me." That was quite an offer for a mother of three teenagers who lived a full hour away with a lot of traffic in between. But she came almost every day. She would arrive about ten in the morning, bringing her daddy a cup of coffee and a donut, and then stay until about two, giving Bob a chance to go out a little. While she was there she would run errands, start dinner, do chores, or just get up on the bed with me and keep me comfortable.

Brad, too, was such a blessing to us in those days, even though he was going through difficult times both professionally and personally. He stopped by whenever he could, just to talk or see what he could do. My son and I have always enjoyed a special bond, and every visit was balm to my spirit.

And that's not even to mention the friends who came to see me, who brought us meals and company, who simply sat with us and talked with us and loved us. My wonderful grandchildren were frequent visitors, and I loved to see the way they were growing. Even with the pain from the shingles, I relished their hugs, drinking in the aliveness of their young bodies.

It was actually a sweet time, that fall after my bone marrow transplant. Bob and I were surrounded by people who love us, buoyed by prayer from friends and colleagues across the nation, and enjoying our new beachside surroundings. We even celebrated our forty-fifth wedding anniversary in October—quietly, with just the family present, but joyfully and full of gratitude that we still had each other.

Not that there weren't a few earthquake rumbles on this part of the journey. I still had my ups and downs, and once I even slipped into a coma after lunch at a restaurant and ended up spending 11 days in the hospital with an infection. The ongoing postherpetic neuralgia was a continual agony as well—and one day I finally told Dr. Barth I couldn't take any more.

He must have seen the desperation in my eyes. "Before you jump out the window," he told me gravely, "give me 24 hours."

Even in my pain, I had to laugh at that. I wasn't quite on the windowsill yet—though it was probably good we had moved to a single-story house!

As a result of that conversation, though, Dr. Barth referred me to a UCLA pain specialist who for the first time was able to make a dent in my discomfort.

Winter came with its rains, then spring with exuberant flowers up and down our block. And our hopes were blooming as well as we began to see the fulfillment of all our prayers for healing. With each month, I felt a little stronger, a little more confident. The earthquake rumbles were fading, and the road we were following through Cancerland started to look more like the normal up-and-down path through life. Though I was still heavily medicated to ward off rejection of my donated cells, still vulnerable to infection, still suffering from the shingles pain, we were also beginning to mark off milestones on the way to healing.

First there was a slight reduction in the lessening pain from the shingles—still bad, but a little better.

Then there was a positive CAT scan in February, and a gradual tapering off of the "chipmunk cheek" medication.

And then came the even bigger milestone of our one-year checkup at the Hutch in Seattle. Tests taken in June of 2001 showed no trace of lymphoma and a 100 percent presence of the donor's bone marrow in my body. I still had a long way to go in my healing, but by all indicators I was cancer free!

In July, for the first time in four years, we were able to attend the Christian Booksellers Association convention in Atlanta, rejoicing to see old friends and be back in circulation.

We also finally received permission to contact my bone marrow donor. Regulations prevent any contact between donor and recipient for at least one year—probably to stave off disappointment in case the transplant doesn't take. But now we were able to contact the donor bank and learn something about this 23-year-old Canadian.

We discovered his name was Dan Rapoi, and that he was a disc jockey in Canada. Then we received word that he was open to talking to us. After a period of phone tag, we finally made a connection. What an amazing thing it was to meet by phone the man whose very cells were moving through my body! My tears flowed as I discovered he is a fine, churchgoing young man who gave God all the credit for the miracle of my healing.

Throughout the next few months, we kept encountering milestones. When Dr. Barth told us in August—after two years of weekly visits—that we didn't need to see him again for a month...we practically jumped for joy.

When my shingles pain subsided another notch in late fall I actually could jump without doubling over.

And then, as we moved into the holiday season, I passed the biggest milestones of all.

First, I made the choice to color my hair—to leave the "sick hair" behind and become my more familiar self. Call it vanity. Call it what you will. But my new "young" hair gave me a new lease on life. Now I was ready to celebrate everything God had done for me.

So I invited my entire family for Thanksgiving—17 of us gathered around the table in our new house, thanking God with everything we had. I hosted a Christmas tea for our new neighbors. And I finally took my turn at hosting the regular Christmas gathering for our special group of friends. For four years my turn had been taken away from me. But now I was ready to break out the lasagna pan, toss the salad with my father's famous olive oil dressing, say a heartfelt blessing, and just have fun!

All that entertaining left me weary but satisfied and deeply grateful. I finally felt I was beginning to recognize the landscape around me.

As I finish this chapter in early 2002 we are still living in that closer-to-normal, milestone-marked region of Cancerland. No major quakes have rocked our world in a while, and although the shingles pain and immunity-suppressing medication are still in my life, they have faded a little into the background. I am walking every day around our neighborhood and enjoying an occasional evening out with friends. Our new home in Newport Beach is a source of joy, although we still miss our beloved Riverside barn. We are taking advantage of our freedom from running the mail-order business to rest, enjoy our family—the whole clan went to Hawaii at Christmas! And I actually hope to begin speaking again sometime this year.

I don't know precisely what I'll say when I finally get on that platform again. But I know it will have something to do with what I've learned on the frightening, earthquake-ridden road through Cancerland.

It was a longer road, a harder road, than I ever expected. It changed my life more profoundly than I was prepared for. But through it all the Lord was there, working through the doctors to heal me, lifting us up on wings of prayer and care, simply wrapping us with his presence when we couldn't even pray, working to prepare us for what will come next in our lives.

It shouldn't have surprised me. After all, he was the one who promised to be with us always.

Even, as I have learned, to Cancerland...and beyond.

DEAR FELLOW TRAVELER,

I don't know what your personal journey has been. I don't know what earthquakes are shaking your foundations, what worries keep you up at night, what pain saps your strength and drags down your spirit.

But I do know one thing. If I could see you at this moment I would hug you tightly and whisper in your ear: You don't have to travel alone.

No matter what road you're traveling—uphill or down, smooth or rocky, even through an earthquake zone—the Lord will be beside you every step of the way. Sometimes you will feel his companionship intensely. Other times you won't know he's been there until you look back and see what he's been doing. Sometimes you will recognize him in the faces of doctors and nurses, friends and family, and sometimes you will encounter him in the lonely places where only you can go.

When you suffer, he will wrap you in his arms.

When your strength gives out, he will carry you.

And even when the ground beneath you seems to shake, he will steady your feet.

With every step you take, he will prepare you for the next step. And no matter where you travel, he will always be in the process of bringing you home.

Put your hand in mine and trust me in this. I've been there. But more important, God is there! If you're going to trust anyone in the land where you're traveling, trust him.

God's richest blessings to you!

Emilie

—☙

GOD'S GIFT OF TRUTH
FOR YOUR OWN JOURNEY

♭ No matter where you travel, God lives there, too. There is nowhere you can go to get away from his love and care.

♭ You can trust the Lord to guide you through every earthquake zone.

♭ To build your faith, remember to look back at where you've been!

—☙

CHAPTER TWO

The Cupboard's Not Bare

Store up for yourselves treasures in heaven, where moth and rust do not destroy, and where thieves do not break in and steal. For where your treasure is, there your heart will be also.

—MATTHEW 6:20

Do not worry, saying, "What shall we eat?" or "What shall we drink?" or "What shall we wear?" For the pagans run after all these things, and your heavenly Father knows that you need them. But seek first his kingdom and his righteousness, and all these things will be given to you as well.

—MATTHEW 6:31-33

2

THE CUPBOARD'S NOT BARE

What I found in my life to carry me through

—☙

Remember that sad old nursery rhyme about poor Mother Hubbard and her hungry dog? She went to fetch him a bone, but "when she got there the cupboard was bare."

I know a little bit about empty cupboards. I grew up in a home where my mother worked day and night to keep body and soul together. And while she always managed to feed us, there were times when our tiny apartment cupboard held little more than a few potatoes and a box of tea.

Maybe that's why I've always loved the idea of a well-stocked, well-organized cupboard. I love being able to open the doors and find an array of neatly arranged boxes and canisters containing not only dog bones (well, maybe Milk Bones) but also rice and pasta and legumes and spices and cans of veggies—everything I need to put together an appealing, nourishing meal on the spur of the moment. I even love the process of stocking a pantry and organizing it and keeping it current. I discovered long ago that a little bit of planning, organization, and maintenance dramatically reduces my stress and gives me a lot of freedom and security.

Planning, organization, and maintenance. In a way, that's the heart of what I've been teaching to women through the years. It's been the central message of my ministry, More Hours in My Day. I've spent a lot of time on speaking platforms showing young women how they can use feather dusters to clean more efficiently, numbered boxes and index cards to organize all the "stuff" in their lives, tea parties and love baskets to enrich their relationships, prayer notebooks and prayer baskets to ensure they had regular quality time with the Lord. And yes, I talked a little bit about how to stock a pantry.

But what I was teaching all those years wasn't just planning, organization, and maintenance—but planning, organization, and maintenance with a purpose. And although I've sold my share of organizing boxes and feather dusters and preorganized prayer notebooks, my purpose was never just to hawk merchandise. My heart was always in showing young women how they could simplify and enrich their lives, how they could make time for what was really important—their families, their relationships, their connection with God—and to be prepared for new opportunities that came their way.

Well, that seems like a long time ago now. It's been a couple of years since I sold a feather duster—and, until recently, since I even used one! So now, after all those years of living and teaching, it seems appropriate to ask, "Did it help? When cancer finally stopped me in my tracks, did any of what I did and taught really make a difference?"

Looking back, I am deeply gratified to realize the answer is yes. When Bob and I faced the challenge of my cancer years, I was thrilled to realize my habits of planning and organization and maintenance paid off in so many ways. When we went to our cupboard, we found it was far from bare.

That's not to say I was ready for cancer! In a sense, we can never be truly prepared for such a time of crisis. I'm not even sure we *should* be completely prepared. Who can live richly and fully while constantly anticipating what might go wrong? There really is a sense that we need to trust God for the future, just as we need to trust him when that future arrives. Jesus told his disciples to not worry about the future, but instead to trust in God's provision.

And yet our same Lord told us to be wakeful and vigilant, watching for what he would bring about in our lives. He told us stories about wise and well-organized virgins who thought ahead to bring oil for their lamps. He reminded us that while we don't know the future, we should always be alert and on the lookout for what is coming. Specifically, he was talking about his own return. But that attitude of watchful waiting, of careful but trusting preparation, applies to the way we live our days and the way we stock our pantries so that we will be ready for whatever the unwrapping of our days reveals.

When hard times hit our family and we had to make difficult decisions under pressure, I found myself thanking heaven for choices I made that stocked our pantries during better days. No, I wasn't perfectly prepared, and I didn't spend every hour of every day getting ready for something that might happen. But when my health failed and our life changed, I was gratified to find that our household was more or less organized, my relationships were in fairly good shape, and the path to my Father's door was well marked and easy to follow.

When our life was rolling along, this state of "more or less" readiness brought me satisfaction and convenience. When crisis came, I believe it helped save my life.

It should be obvious by now, of course, that I'm not talking about my literal pantry. I'm talking instead about physical, emotional, and spiritual provisions that can carry us through difficult periods in our lives.

These include the daily habits and practices that just make life easier—such as having a place for everything and tackling big jobs in bite-sized segments (15 minutes a day!). They involve efforts to bring beauty into our lives—such as arranging a beautiful tea tray or putting together a love basket for a friend or taking the time to create a pleasing environment in our homes. Relationship investments—such as writing a note to a friend who is hurting or making peace after an argument instead of letting disagreements fester— bring bounty to anyone's pantry. And even more important are those habits and disciplines that keep us close to God— setting aside time for regular prayer and Scripture reading, practicing trust in the Lord and obedience to him.

Again and again during the four years I was fighting cancer, Bob and I found that our "pantry" shelves contained the provisions we needed to make it through our wearying and complicated days and weeks.

Household organizational skills, for instance, paid off when we had to pack up with little notice and move—three times, and while I was physically depleted. Items we used often were clean and in their places, ready to pack and move. Seldom-used possessions were already packed in boxes and labeled, with their contents listed on index cards. Unwanted items had already been disposed of. We knew

exactly where all our vital paperwork was, so we didn't
have to dig through piles and boxes just to do our necessary
business. Current addresses were near at hand, so notifying
people of our address change was a painless proposition.
We had savings we could draw on when our income
dropped dramatically.

When I came back from my bone marrow transplant
and immediately faced the task of closing up a house where
we had lived for 30 years, I was doubly glad we had taken
the time and trouble to get organized and stay organized.
It's hard enough to move and even harder to downsize a
household, especially when you're still sick and weak. To
add 30 years of accumulated junk piled in closets, drawers,
attic, and garage—not to mention cleaning to get the house
ready to sell—would have completely overwhelmed my
Bob and me.

So many other habits, little and large, proved to be valuable pantry items when Bob and I were coping with my
cancer. My practice of stockpiling blank notecards and
stamps, for instance, helped us keep in touch with the dear
people who wrote us and called us. For although there were
days when I couldn't pick up a pen, there were also days
when I could manage a quick note—but not a trip out of the
house to buy a card. Being prepared helped boost my spirits
when I was discouraged about not being able to do _any-
thing_. And on the days when I couldn't write, Bob made use
of our cache of cards to keep track of our correspondence.

Here's another way I discovered that years of pantry
stocking paid off. It may sound a little odd in light of my
illness, but I really am convinced that my years-long habit
of healthy eating and regular exercise served me well in
these years when my body was fighting for its life. It's true
that healthy eating and exercise didn't _prevent_ cancer, and
my insistence on natural treatment may actually have

delayed a diagnosis. But I am convinced that years of taking care of my body gave it the underlying strength to survive the hours of treatment and rebound when given a chance. In addition, my habit of doing what is necessary to take care of my health carried over into a willingness to do what was necessary to be healed—even when the treatments themselves were unpleasant.

Even more valuable than these practical habits, I discovered, were the relationships I had managed to maintain over the years. It wasn't always easy, when our schedule was impossibly busy, to set aside time for buying gifts, writing cards, sharing visits, and even enjoying tea or coffee with friends both near and far away. After a hard day of speaking in a faraway city, we were often tempted to retreat to our hotel room instead of opening our hearts to new friendships with our hosts. Closer to home, Bob and I often found it painful and difficult to work through thorny relationships both in our own close family and in our wider family circles. It's wasn't easy for the two of us to learn to forgive each other and put up with each other and talk out our problems and keep on trying even when we were fed up. It wasn't easy for either of us to set aside bitterness and resentment toward family members who had hurt us in the past (in my case, my alcoholic father and my manipulative aunt and my abusive uncle) but were no longer around to confront.

There were times, in the past, when maintaining the bonds of friendship and family ties took all my grace and all our patience. But how many times during these painful cancer years have I raised my hands to heaven to thank the Lord for the beautiful and healing relationships stored in our living "pantry."

When I read the gifts and cards that flew in from across the nation, full of prayers and Scriptures and sincere good wishes, how I thanked God I had taken time to build relationships as well as business contacts—to speak with women after conferences instead of just collapsing in a hotel room, to answer letters from people who had liked my books, to get to know our publishing colleagues as brothers and sisters in Christ and not just sources of contracts and royalty checks.

When old and new friends in Newport Beach—people like Yoli and Bob Brogger—gathered around us to pray and read Scripture and anoint me with oil, I was grateful for the many notes and phone calls and visits that had kept those friendships alive over the years.

When I lay motionless on the couch, nauseated and in pain, and watched my friend Donna Otto scrub my kitchen (the night before she had cheerfully cleaned up much worse), I luxuriated in the comfort of a friendship we had nurtured for so long, even though we had never lived in the same state.

When my brother Edmond visited our home or my only cousin Phillip stood by my hospital bedside and prayed for me, I was grateful for my efforts to maintain ties with my sometimes dysfunctional Jewish family. Eddie and I spent more time together during the past few years than we ever had before, and we worked together to get a plaque for our mother's grave. Phillip has gone through so much over the years, but he has also given his life to Christ and worked hard to stay connected to Bob and me.

My visits with these precious relatives during my illness were definitely a balm to my spirit. And so was the knowledge that I had long ago made my peace with hurtful members of my family who were now deceased. The work I had put into laying aside bitterness and anger toward these difficult people in my life and forgiving them now paid enormous dividends. Instead of spending my limited energy on dealing with past pain, I was able to focus all my energy positively—on loving and healing.

And how much more, on days when I was weary or lonely or discouraged, did I reap the benefit of time and effort I had put into nurturing relationships in my own close family—my husband and children and grandchildren. When I felt my Jenny's embrace, felt her loving tears on my face, I rejoiced over the hard-won patience and forgiveness that had brought our once-difficult relationship to the point of such love and harmony and support. When I heard my son's familiar voice on the phone or at our door, felt his strong arms and felt his strong support, I rejoiced in the special connection that has always kept Brad and me close. When I luxuriated in my grandchildren's freshness and enthusiasm and enjoyed their unselfish giving, I rejoiced in our efforts to keep in touch, to invite them over on a regular basis, to play with them and teach them and share with them.

And Bob—as I watched my Bob day after day, marveling at how much he sacrificed to take care of me, drawing on his strength and patience, I knew that every effort either of us had ever made to strengthen and build our marriage was infinitely worthwhile. For 40 years we had worked to build a relationship that would stand the test of time. For 40 years we had tried to take the healthy path instead of the easy one—to talk out our differences, forgive each other our shortcomings, weather our storms, balance our roles, keep our romance alive, make sure our relationship was centered on Christ.

Our efforts to stay connected to others, I was finding, are almost never wasted. Yes, there were friends who didn't show up when things got tough for us. There were carefully nurtured relationships that faded to nothing. But there were so many more relationships that proved as energizing as food and water, as healing as medicine. So many friends and acquaintances called and wrote and brought dinner and prayed for us.

I believe to the depths of my being that the time and effort I put into stocking my pantry with loving relationships helped save my life. At the very least, it helped me build a capacity for love and friendship that would help keep my spirit open and optimistic at a time when pain and fear tempted me to pull in on myself. My relationships didn't take away the pain and fear and illness, but they carried me through these things on a lovely cloud of caring. I can honestly say that, until I had cancer, I never knew just how much I was loved.

I've come to believe, in fact, that the relationships we nurture in the course of living our life are second in importance only to the relationship we build with God. And oh, what a worthwhile thing it is to stock a pantry with intimate knowledge of the Father, the Son, and the Holy Spirit. In these difficult, painful cancer years, I felt my life-enhancing spiritual connections become truly life saving.

For long periods during my illness, my eyes wouldn't focus correctly and I couldn't read. And yet there were so many sleepless, painful nights when Scripture I had studied years before came floating back to soothe my troubled spirit. So many afternoons when I was heavily medicated and could barely stay awake—but the psalms Bob read me still sifted through my deadened senses. So many mornings when a bad medical report was countered with the scriptural knowledge that no matter what happened, all would be well.

Years of coming to the Lord in prayer made it easy to fall on my spiritual knees even when my mind was sluggish and my body could barely move. Years of trusting him even in difficulty made it easier to trust him when our days were filled with dread and death seemed to loom close. Years of learning to obey the Spirit's promptings helped both Bob and me move forward and make decisions when we needed to instead of stewing endlessly over our confusing options. Years of getting to know him on an intimate level made it easier to recognize him even in those dreary hospital corridors—and to cling to him in my pain instead of pulling away in anger and doubt.

How grateful I am for the years I spent organizing my spiritual disciplines to make them easier to follow, harder to let slide—my "15 minute a day" habit that prompted me to pray even when I didn't think I had time; my prayer basket, which provided a visual reminder that I needed time with the Lord; my prayer notebook, which helped focus my scattered thoughts and pray more faithfully. How I hope that my teaching inspired (and will inspire) others to stock their spiritual pantries with such treasures, ready for the day when they will so desperately need them.

Even as Bob and I have relied on the provisions in our pantry, however, we have been increasingly aware that we weren't the only ones who stocked it! We did our part, but preparing for the future wasn't entirely up to us—and I think that's vital to realize.

Our Lord provides. He knows what we need the most, what we're going to need in the future, when we're going to need it. And I believe he is constantly at work preparing us for the future, even when we are unaware of what he is doing in our lives. That's not to say we shouldn't plan or organize or maintain—but we must never forget who is really in charge of our future.

I can see that more clearly than ever as I look back over the past six years. In so many ways, the Lord was stocking my pantry with the physical, emotional, and spiritual resources I would need to make it through my cancer years.

With the kind of ingenuity that only the Creator of the universe and the Lord of our days can muster, he was making use of our experiences, even the negative ones, to prepare my whole family for what lay ahead.

During those terrible early years of Jenny's separation and divorce, for example, God was working in my entire family to prepare us all to face much more difficult circumstances.

My Bob, for instance, who by nature is an impatient man, was gradually learning to wait on God to resolve the painful matter of Jenny's divorce. He was learning to hold his tongue even when others (such as Jenny) violated his high standards and to let God handle his anger and indignation. He was becoming more flexible, more humble, more willing to love unconditionally. And how we would need those qualities when he had to take over all my household responsibilities, sit for hours by my bedside, and continually show his love for a wife who didn't have any strength to do much in return.

Jenny, who had been so desperately unhappy and insecure that she had been willing to risk her family and her soul in a search for fulfillment, was finally able to listen to the Lord's call in her life. She was finally beginning to understand both the need for repentance and the Lord's gigantic mercy, to acknowledge who she was—a child of God—and who she wanted to be—a good mother and a woman of God. She was finally able to trust God enough to put him in charge of her future. And as these things began to happen in her life, she began maturing into a more focused, more unselfish person. The woman who prayed over me and cared for me in my illness, who thought of creative ways to help and who rallied her troops to the cause of supporting her parents was simply not the same woman who had fled her unhappy marriage. Even through the agonizing experiences of her divorce and its aftermath, she was being prepared for what was to come.

And I, too, was being prepared by this terrible event that disrupted our lives. The Lord used my sessions of praying Scripture over Jenny to strengthen my own patience, my trust, my endurance, my understanding of God's sovereignty, and my willingness to obey him. For three long years I walked the canal near our home, praying for Jenny's situation to change. What happened, instead, was that *I* changed. In three years of walking and praying, I gradually became more willing to listen to God, more willing to let him be in control of what was happening in our lives, to trust him for the outcome instead of telling him how and when it should be done. How much I would need that spirit of trust in the years when my diagnosis kept changing, when solutions seemed to elude my doctors and our prayers for healing just didn't seem to work.

I truly believe that God used the circumstances of Jenny's divorce to prepare Jenny, Bob, and me to withstand the circumstances of my illness. But please understand— that doesn't mean the divorce *had* to happen or that it was a good thing for her to leave her husband. I would never suggest that God planned for our family to go through the agony of that divorce just to prepare us for the agony of my cancer!

God is sovereign. He knows the end from the beginning. But he also gives us the freedom to say no to him, and that freedom often gets us in trouble. We fail. We rebel. We cause ourselves and others endless pain and heartache.

Yet God is also an amazing, creative, redemptive God who uses even the raw material of the messes we make— along with our willingness to repent and come back to him—to provide for us. Like a mother teaching her child to knit, he picks up our dropped stitches, puts them back on the needle, and manages to work our mistakes into the beautiful fabric of the whole. And in the process, he even manages to prepare us for future projects.

And often, of course, God's provision is more direct. Rather than use our experiences to prepare us for a crisis, he gives us manna in the midst of our need. As I look back on my cancer years, I can see so many instances where God's direct provision was timely and just right.

When I realize, for example, that Bob was not sick—not once!—in the four years that I had cancer, I can only marvel. Bob has never been a paragon of good health. I (the health food nut) have often scolded him about eating the wrong foods, not getting enough exercise, being too impatient. The last few years have put him under tremendous stress, day after day. And yet since my illness my Bob has not had a cold to pass along to me. He has never suffered a case of flu that would keep him from his household duties (I imagine he sometimes wished for *something* that would do that!). What a loving and surprising provision the Lord made for us in Bob's ongoing good health!

Another example of God's direct provision for us is the availability of our new house in Newport Beach. What are the chances that in an incredibly tight real estate market, in an area where most houses are either too large, too small, inappropriately designed, or simply too expensive, the perfect house for us would show up at the perfect moment and at a price we could afford—and even before the Riverside house sold? The house is one-story, with no stairs to vex Bob's creaky knees or my still-weak condition. There is a secluded guest room where friends and grandkids can visit, where my editor can come and work. And the ocean, my constant source of peace and inspiration, is just a few blocks away.

Even in small ways, the Lord continued to sustain us directly during the course of my cancer. A friend would stop by with a pot of soup on an evening when Bob was too worn out to cook. My favorite cot would be available when I showed up for a session of chemo. A bird outside our balcony would lift my spirits when I could barely lift my head.

God does provide. That's the most important thing to keep in mind as we are thinking about what we need now and what we will need in the future. We can depend on our loving heavenly Father to accomplish his purposes in our lives and in our world. He will use our habits and our disciplines to keep us close to him. He will work through our experiences to prepare us for what we need. He will dispense his daily manna to carry us through. He is...and will be...the source of all good things in our lives.

This is not to say we shouldn't plan, organize, maintain—that we shouldn't do what we can to manage our lives and prepare for the future. In fact, one of the most profound lessons my illness has taught me is that it's important to do these things *now* instead of waiting for a better day. Time is short, and we don't know what will happen to us tomorrow. So it's important not to wait until tomorrow to put those photos in an album or file those insurance papers or call that friend or have that quiet time. Do it now. Better yet, *start* doing it and keep at it 15 minutes a day!

But all is not lost if you neglect to do these things—if you don't get around to the photos or if you stuff the insurance papers in a drawer or even if you put off that quiet time until tomorrow. God is a redeeming God, and his provision doesn't depend on our being organized! One way or another, if you depend on him, he is going to bring you where you need to be.

And this brings us back to the paradox—that even as we're planning and organizing and maintaining, we need to keep waiting on the Lord, depending on him, giving up our anxiety for the future and keeping an eye open for miracles of provision. So how do we do that—live in daily dependence but prepare watchfully at the same time?

I think we do it by stocking our pantries primarily with the kinds of things that moth and rust cannot corrupt. Not just sugar and kidney beans, but trust and thankfulness and obedience. Not just boxes of tea, but habits of courage and self-discipline. Not just spices and staples, but carefully nurtured relationships both with other people and with our heavenly Father.

In the meantime, there's no reason we shouldn't stock our actual pantries—or that we shouldn't use our feather dusters or enjoy tea with our friends. I would say the very opposite. Prepare yourself as best you can for your life—but remember it's all for a purpose. By all means, stock up on staples, making sure you have enough on hand to entertain angels at the spur of the moment—and then don't be stingy with the invitations. Use your feather duster regularly so that your home feels like a haven to those you love and welcomes strangers for a touch of holy hospitality.

Such daily disciplines walk hand in hand with the biblical principles of being ready for whatever the Lord brings into our lives as well as making the most of the time he gives us and depending on him daily for provision. If we do them for the right purposes, they actually become a way of storing up treasures in heaven—filling our physical, emotional, and spiritual pantries with faith, hope, love, and the eternal presence of the Lord, who really does provide.

Dear Friend in Christ,

If you haven't faced a crisis or time of difficulty yet in your life, take a deep breath—you will. The good news is that you can depend on the Lord to provide for you in time of need. God will often use our own experiences and our own characters as raw materials for his provision, and very little of what you do to prepare yourself will be wasted. From my own experience with battling cancer, here are some ways I suggest you can plan, organize, and maintain to make better use of the Lord's provision.

- Spend some time organizing your "life pantries" so that you know what you have in your household and your life. Store what you want so that you can easily retrieve it, and get rid of extraneous "stuff" that just gets in the way.

- Do some basic planning for illness or disaster. Do you have a will or a similar document, such as a trust? Is your insurance adequate? Does someone besides you know where your important information is—and can it be quickly located?

- Take care of your relationships—you need them now, and you may really need them later. Pay special attention to everyday maintenance (cards, phone calls) and make peace with those with whom you've had conflicts.

- Stock up on positive habits and attitudes. Try to learn to tackle tasks without procrastinating and face problems instead of hiding from them. Learn to let go of bitterness—you'll need that skill for survival someday. Learn to face problems and act even when you're afraid.

♭ Place a priority on staying current with the Lord. Spend time with him every day, even if all you can manage is an extra-long bathroom break! Confess your sins to him regularly and accept his forgiveness. Practice trusting his provision and obeying him. The more you say yes to the Lord's voice, the easier it'll be to hear him.

♭ Write down your memories of what God has done for you in the past and how he has answered prayer. Write them down in a notebook or computer program so you can refer back to them easily. You'll be surprised at how encouraging such a "spiritual memory book" can be.

You don't have to do it all in a day, but don't put it off! You never know what tomorrow will bring. You do know who is in charge of tomorrow, though. As long as you're in the Lord's company, your cupboard will never be bare.

God's richest provision to you!

Emilie

GOD'S GIFT OF TRUTH
FOR YOUR TIME OF NEED

- In God's economy, nothing that happens to you is ever wasted.

- Planning, organization, and maintenance can help make your hard times easier.

- Relationships—with God and with others— are the most important treasures you can stock up in your life.

- Time is short. Don't put off doing what you know to do.

- God can use even your negative experiences for his good purposes.

- Don't worry! When you open your hands in need—even if you've neglected to prepare— God will not let you down.

CHAPTER THREE

Leaning in the Long Hours

How long, O LORD? Will you forget me forever? How long will you hide your face from me? How long must I wrestle with my thoughts and every day have sorrow in my heart?...But I trust in your unfailing love; my heart rejoices in your salvation. I will sing to the LORD, for he has been good to me.

—PSALM 13:1-2, 5-6

I wait for the LORD, my soul waits, and in his word I put my hope. My soul waits for the Lord more than watchmen wait for the morning, more than the watchmen wait for the morning.

—PSALM 130:5-6

Yet the LORD longs to be gracious to you; he rises to show you compassion. For the LORD is a God of justice. Blessed are all who wait for him!

—ISAIAH 30:18-19

3

LEANING IN THE LONG HOURS

Reluctant lessons of waiting and pain

—⚬—

I knew cancer would be a difficult experience. But I wasn't quite prepared for just how *tedious* an experience it would be!

I once read that moviemaking involves brief moments of high drama interspersed with long items of total boredom. Anyone who has lived through cancer treatment knows that description applies to us, too.

There are those few high-drama moments—when you first hear your diagnosis, when your test results are especially good or bad, when you have a bad reaction to medication or a breakthrough in treatment. In between, though, you spend the majority of your time cooling your heels in waiting rooms, relaxing in recliners while IVs pump chemicals into your system, or just lying on the couch while you wait for your strength to build. Sometimes you can't focus or concentrate, which means you can't read, and even watching TV can be a struggle. Sometimes you have sores in your mouth and food tastes terrible, so you can't talk or eat much. Your immune system may be compromised, so you can't really go out in public. In addition to being miserable, a lot of the time you're just bored and frustrated.

For caregivers, I think, the tedium and frustration of waiting can be even tougher. For the duration of my illness, my Bob, who is a very active, social person, was practically under house arrest. He yearned to go out to eat, to go to movies, to spend time with friends or just take long walks through the town. Instead, he spent the majority of his time sitting by my bedside or puttering around the house while I slept. And, of course, he chauffeured me to all those endless waiting rooms and waited with me there.

For both of us, the experience of waiting, waiting, waiting was one of the hardest aspects of my cancer years. That's not surprising, because waiting is one of the hardest things any of us has to do in our lives. It's also an unavoidable part of being human and a built-in aspect of being a Christian. It's no wonder so many passages in the Bible speak about enduring and being patient. We need those qualities because from the time we are small, it seems, we are *always* waiting—

- for school to be out
- for suppertime
- to "get big"
- not to be grounded anymore
- to drive and vote
- to finish our degree and get a job

- to find the right mate

- for the baby to arrive

- for the promotion to materialize

- for the loan to go through

- for promises to be kept

- for our prayers to be answered...

When things are going well, we wait for them to get better. When times are hard, we wait for circumstances to improve. We wait for good things in anticipation and frustration. We wait for bad things in dread...and frustration. And when we are ill or in trouble, the waiting can be simply excruciating. We sit in chairs at the doctor's or the lawyer's or the tax accountant's or toss and turn in the middle of the night. Waiting for a diagnosis. For a resolution. For it all to be over. For the pain to let up just a little. For morning. Sometimes just for the Lord to just end our suffering and call us home.

Jesus once said that in this world we would have trouble.

He didn't specifically add, but experience tells us, that a lot of our trouble would involve waiting!

The trouble, of course, is that most of us don't really like to wait. I don't. Bob _really_ doesn't! We have both been active people all our lives. We've always liked to take care of business, to make plans, to do it now, to do _something_. To be placed in so many situations where waiting was our only real choice was sometimes frustrating, sometimes depressing, sometimes downright excruciating.

Why is waiting so hard? Sometimes it's because we want the outcome so badly. We want the flowers to bloom, the baby to come, the prayers of our deepest heart to be answered—and answered with a yes! We're like a little child anticipating her birthday, our heart jumping up and down with excitement—we just can't wait for the good times to roll. We want our pain to stop, our troubles to cease, and we can just taste how sweet our life will be when that finally happens.

But waiting can also be hard when we fear what we're waiting for—the expected pink slip, the IRS audit, the biopsy results. We may feel like a child who has broken a vase and is waiting for punishment—wondering which will be worse, the waiting or the outcome.

A long period of waiting can be especially difficult because it tends to push our abandonment buttons. Even when we know better, waiting tends to make us feel bereft and unloved. When we've prayed and waited and prayed and we're still waiting, it's easy to give in to the feeling that God doesn't care, that he has left us to our fate, that our waiting will never end.

But I think the biggest reason waiting is hard is that it takes away our illusions of control. It interrupts our plans and our schedules and punctures our sense that we can run our lives the way we think best. Our spirits rebel against this reminder that our time is not our own and that a lot of what happens is outside our power.

To make things worse, waiting confuses our sense of what we can and can't do. When we're in waiting mode, we don't know how to plan. We resist starting something new because we don't know if we'll be able to finish. And if we do start something, we have trouble concentrating because we're wondering when the phone will ring or when our name will be called or when the symptoms will start again.

As I said, I really don't like to wait. After years of practice, I don't like it much better than I did before, though my times of waiting are far from over. (For a cancer survivor, regular checks for recurrences are just a part of life.) And yet I've discovered that there is good to be found in those painful, frustrating waiting times. The longer I live, in fact, the more I see God's work in our world, the more clearly I can see God's purposes in much of our waiting. Our sovereign Lord truly knows the end from the beginning, and his timing is perfect. I love the way the old gospel song puts it: "He might not come when you want him, but he's right on time!"

How can all that frustrating waiting serve God's purpose?

One thing I know it can do is make us ready for whatever comes next. Waiting whets our appetites for the time when the waiting is over and we finally see the unfolding of God's promises. Sometimes we're so ready that we're willing to do whatever it takes—even something frightening or unpleasant—just to end the waiting!

If you've ever been pregnant, you know what I'm talking about. I once heard it said that God gives us those last few weeks of pregnancy to make labor seem worth it! A woman nearing the end of her term just can't wait to hold that baby in her arms, and she's so tired of being pregnant she's willing to do almost anything. That kind of incentive, born of waiting, can be just what we need to overcome our natural resistance to change and move forward with what God wants to do next with our life.

Here's another thing waiting can do for us: it can bring us out of childishness to maturity. In fact, waiting is one of the important lessons children must learn if they want to be mature adults. Instead of screaming to get their way "right now," they learn to wait their turn or defer to their parents' judgment. They learn that there is a time for dinner, a time for snacks, a time to play, a time to go to bed. They learn to give up something good today in favor of something even better another day.

It's true that not *every* child learns these lessons well and that most adults continue to struggle with grown-up versions of these same issues. But that's precisely my point. Even as adults, we are still being matured by God, and I believe he uses our waiting times as part of that process. As we wait, if we let him, the Lord will make us stronger, wiser, more patient, more enduring. More mature. More fit for the kingdom.

Another thing waiting does—or can do, if we let it—is teach us our limits and adjust our perspective. It reminds us of who we are and who God is, and it helps us see our circumstances more clearly.

In my own times of waiting, I've discovered that my priorities seem to shift. Little things that once seemed insignificant loom large, while issues I thought were crucial lose their sense of urgency. I find myself focusing on the moment, on what I can do to make life better for myself and others, and letting God take care of the big picture. My life has become simpler, not by my design, but by his design. I have a better sense of what's important and what isn't—what really needs to be done now and what can wait.

Maybe what's really happening in these times is that waiting gives me a chance to draw closer to God and see things his way. I think one of the most basic and most important things our times of waiting can do is drive us into the arms of our heavenly Father. Sometimes, when the waiting becomes unbearable, all we can do is run into his open arms and just cuddle up. This is not the same thing as giving up! In fact, I found it's the best way to keep on going. I learned to spend so many of my waiting hours, especially the ones when I couldn't read or eat or talk and could barely move, in the Lord's presence, just being, feeling his nearness and his love, leaning on him and trusting him to do what was best.

In the meantime, of course, God was doing his work behind the scenes—and this points to another purpose in our waiting: to let necessary events unfold that will bring us to the right conclusion. God always sees the big picture, and I believe that many times his primary purpose in our waiting is to simply weave the strands of our circumstances together in the way that will be best for us and for the furtherance of his kingdom.

This happened again and again during the years of my illness, although we usually couldn't see it happening just then. All the time we were waiting and waiting for a correct diagnosis, for instance, and then waiting some more for the chemo and radiation and antibiotics to work in my body, the medical community was making rapid strides in understanding the nature of my particular cancer and the ways it could be treated. The cutting edge treatment for MALT-cell lymphoma actually moved ahead faster than the progress of my disease! And during this same time, God was at work in the heart of Dan Rapoi, prompting him to be tested as a bone marrow donor. Out of all my blood relatives, my friends and acquaintances, and all the other donors in databases around the world, Dan turned out to be the only perfect match. He was there just when I needed him, able and willing to go through the procedure and essentially save my life.

Then in Seattle, while Bob and I waited for the transplant to take effect and tried to make a decision on selling our Riverside house, God was working to provide the perfect house for us in Newport Beach. We had contacted a real estate agent just to see what was out there, and one day she called to say, "I've found your house, and it's everything you want, but you need to make a bid today because it won't be there tomorrow." Bob had used the waiting time to get our affairs in order, and we were able to make the bid that day. To be able to concentrate my energies on healing instead of house hunting was a true gift and an example of the Lord's remarkable timing.

Again and again in my life, I've seen periods of waiting serve God's purposes—teaching, strengthening, revealing truth. But it's important to recognize that waiting doesn't automatically do these things!

If we let it, waiting can make us bitter and angry. It can lead us to take matters into our own hands and make a mess of things or to just give up hoping. As in so many areas of our lives, God gives us the choice of how we respond to our circumstances. Whether we grow stronger in our waiting or simply grow more weary depends largely on our willingness to wait positively, which mostly means to lean close to him during our waiting times and trust him to do his work through and behind our waiting.

But as we've seen, that's not easy. How can we remain positive when our thumbs are sore from twiddling and we've begun to wonder if we'll ever see an end to our waiting?

One thing that helps, I've found, is to keep reminding yourself what you're *really* waiting for—which is for God to do his work in your life. This is true whether you're waiting for a new baby or a new job, for your illness to be healed or your grief to lessen a little, for a husband to come to his senses or a wayward child to come back home. As humans, we don't get to predetermine what the outcome of our waiting will be, and the more we can remember this, the more frustration we can save.

I have found that the only kind of hope that is healthy to give up in life is the hope of being in charge and getting our own way. This is so hard for most of us to get through our heads. We're perfectly happy telling the Lord of the universe to wait for us—we'll get around to his agenda when we're not so busy. Then we get antsy when we're forced to wait on the Lord. How backward is that? Who do we think we are?

Another key to waiting positively, I've found, is to keep on participating in life even while you're waiting. This isn't easy. When you're waiting for something to happen, your mind is focused on the possible outcome, and this makes you restless. It's hard to settle down and take care of ordinary business when part of you is waiting for the phone to ring. And yet the bills still need to be paid. Children still need to be hugged, to be taken to school. The kitchen can be cleaned, resumes can be sent out, the garden can be weeded. Life doesn't stop simply because part of you is in a holding pattern. You don't know how long your waiting will take, so it just makes sense to take care of your business as best you can, trusting God to take care of what you can't manage.

In such circumstances, I've found that it helps to think in small increments. I don't have control over tomorrow, but I can choose what I'm going to do in the next ten minutes. What am I going to do with life right now? Is it going to count?

In the midst of our waiting periods, I've found God often has specific work for us to do—work we might never accomplish if we weren't knocked off our regular schedule for a waiting period. Even in an actual hospital waiting room, there is more productive work to do than reading a year-old magazine. You can strike a blow for life by knitting baby blankets for the neonatal unit of a hospital or crocheting hats for a local shelter. You can improve your mind or lift your spirits by reading Scripture. You can do what Bob does and write out a devotion on a big index card. Or you can ease tension by smiling at your fellow waiters or entertaining a bored child.

If your waiting is longer, there is still a lot you can do. Your current circumstances may give you more time than ever to pray or to listen. Ask the Lord to show you what jobs he has for you to do while you're waiting. Ask him to show you some of the purpose and possibilities in your pain—realizing that you probably won't see the whole picture until it's all over.

Bob and I, for instance, have been amazed at the ways God used us during the long, slow days when I was undergoing therapy and then moving toward recovery. Again and again he brought people into our life who needed to be recognized, who needed to be loved and listened to, who needed someone to take an interest in them, who needed to hear the Good News of Christ. We met them at the hospital, at the cancer clinic, on the shuttle buses, in the hotel lobby. And hard as it was to focus outside our own set of problems, we always found blessing when we managed to reach out to them in some way. We tried to make a point of learning their names, asking about their families, giving them copies of our books if we thought that was appropriate, slipping them little notes of encouragement.

Bob, especially, was able to do amazing things during his long period of enforced idleness. He took care of the big matters of our finances and our business. He managed the little details of cooking, cleaning, and eating. He wrote five books during this time, writing in small snatches during my naps. (I know he's been listening to me all these years, because the technique he evolved is basically writing inspirational literature in 15 minutes a day!) And whenever he could, he made friends with the people around us. I'm sure the staff of the Marriott Residence Inn—not to mention my fellow patients—were sad to see my friendly, caring husband go.

One of the true keys to positive waiting, of course, is to consciously wait on the Lord. If you are physically up to it and time permits, you can read and study Scripture. You can almost always pray—asking God not only to bring a good outcome, but to bring his blessings to your time of waiting. When you invite the Lord into your waiting, you open yourself to being shaped and molded by him instead of giving in to anger and frustration and bitterness.

Bob and I especially found comfort in the psalms during our long waiting periods. In fact, we found that the psalms are almost a user's manual on how to wait on the Lord. So is the book of Job, which reads like a short story about the most painful waiting imaginable, and some of the prophets, who spoke comfort to a nation waiting to return to their homeland.

All of these portions of the Bible reminded us that it's all right to complain—even loudly—about how much we hurt and how hard it is to wait. Many of the psalms consist almost entirely of moans and gripes and complaints, some directed at God. And the psalmists apparently weren't too concerned about always keeping a positive attitude! (Some of the psalms start out so whiny they almost embarrass me!) Job, too, chose to speak his heart to the Lord and to state outright his contention that he had been treated unfairly. I learned from these Scriptures that being honest with God about how we feel is one of the ways we open our lives to his work.

But these Scriptures also show something else. It's all right to voice your complaints—even loudly—while you are waiting…as long as you let the Lord bring you back around to an understanding of who's in charge. That's exactly what happens in Job and in the "moaning and complaining" psalms. Job and the psalmists express their feelings honestly to God, not holding back. They trust him with their feelings. And then, still trusting, they let him lead them back around to realization of who God is and who they are. And when that happens, their only possible response is praise!

Trusting the Lord. That, I believe, is truly the essence of what we can learn while we wait and what will carry us through the waiting. In the Bible, whenever it says to wait, what it's usually saying is "trust." It's saying: "Remember who's in charge here, and remember what he's like. He's come through in the past, and he'll come through again. His way is best." And of course we know that's true—though it takes a lot of waiting and a lot of fulfillment to teach us that at a heart level.

What we're really waiting for, even when we don't know it, is for God to work out his purposes on earth. He has reasons for making us wait—reasons that have to do with what he wants us to become and how his timing needs to unfold.

I think it helps to remember that God has built a certain amount of waiting into creation. He does everything in due season, and one thing has to happen before another does. Seed must be buried and plants need to grow before fruit can appear. Humans must go through childhood before they can become men and women. And the truth we have to get through our heads is that living the life God has dreamed for each of us, bearing fruit in God's own season, is a process that can't be hurried. There's not much we can do about this fact but cooperate, try to keep calm, do what we know to do—and wait for God to bring everything to fulfillment.

The closer we can come to linking our desires with his purposes, the more bearable I believe our waiting will become. But I don't think he wants the wait to be *too* bearable. Then we would become complacent and stop growing, and we would lose some of our desire for the full coming of his kingdom. He wants us to wait in peace, trusting him and leaning on him, but also with open-eyed anticipation, still looking forward, our eyes on the doorway to the future.

Always waiting for the time when all our waiting will be over, and we rejoice to hear the Father call our name.

DEAR WAITING-ROOM COMPANION,

I don't have to ask if you're waiting for something because I *know* you are—and how well I know the frustration that can keep your thumbs twiddling and your feet tapping and your soul on edge! I only hope you can take some comfort, as I have learned to do, from the knowledge that even as you wait, God is at work.

As far as I can tell, we don't have a choice about waiting, but we have a choice about how we wait. We can wait in bitterness and resignation, or we can wait in hope. But if we believe in God and trust him, hope is the only logical choice.

If waiting is getting you down, perhaps you need to pray not for an end to the waiting, but for the tools to carry you through. Pray for strength, endurance, and patience. Pray for insight about what you're really waiting for and guidance as to what God wants you to do in the meantime.

And all the time that you're waiting, keep your eyes open for all that the Lord is going to bring to fruition in your life.

The Lord's peace to you,

Emilie

—੭

GOD'S GIFT OF TRUTH
FOR YOUR WAITING TIMES

ƥ Your waiting has a purpose, even if you can't always see it. Even while you're cooling your heels, waiting for an outcome, God is at work. Trust that!

ƥ Life doesn't stop while you're waiting on the Lord. There's always something you can do while you wait.

ƥ When all you can do is wait...*lean*. Imagine yourself in the Father's strong arms. (You are.) Watch with him. Wait with him.

—੭

CHAPTER FOUR

Lord of the Locust Years

The LORD gave and the LORD has taken away; may the name of the LORD be praised.

—JOB 1:21

So I will restore to you the years that the swarming locust has eaten....You shall eat in plenty and be satisfied, And praise the name of the LORD your God, Who has dealt wondrously with you; And My people shall never be put to shame.

—JOEL 2:25-26 NKJV

4

Lord of the Locust Years

What I gained when I lost so much

—❧—

Once upon a time there was a woman whose life was busy and happy and fulfilling. She loved the Lord, loved her husband of 40 years, loved her two grown children, and absolutely doted on her five grandchildren. Home was important to her, so she spent much of her considerable energy feathering her cozy nest—her dream house, where she and her husband had lived and worked for 30 years. But she also had the privilege of traveling around the country, speaking to large groups of women and seeing God work through her words and ministry.

She wasn't a millionaire, but she made a good living through speaking and writing books and operating a mail-order business. (Her husband managed her business and shared in her ministry.) And though she wasn't a spring chicken, people found her attractive, and she did her best to help nature along with a healthy diet and plenty of exercise. Her eyes were clear and bright, her walk quick and energetic. She enjoyed shopping in thrift shops and antique malls, busying herself around the house, and gathering family and good friends around her for a simple meal or an elaborate formal tea.

Do you recognize this woman? I used to know her well. Unfortunately, I'll probably never see her again—at least not the way she used to be.

Four years later, you see, almost everything about this woman had changed. She still loved the Lord, and she loved her family more than ever. But all her speaking engagements had been canceled, the business had been sold, and her husband, who worked with her, was out of a job as well. (He also lost his chief cook and housekeeper and had to take on most of these duties himself.) Their income had dropped dramatically just as huge new expenses loomed. Their dream house was on the market. As for her looks and her health and her strength and her freedom—these things had all but vanished. She could barely remember what it was like to live a day without pain. And her old life—the energetic, high-producing old life—seemed like a dim memory.

Have you ever had a time like that, when you felt that your life was being pared down to the bare essentials and perhaps beyond? That's what the experience of cancer can be like. So can a number of other life experiences: a bereavement, a serious accident, a divorce, a job loss. Even a life passage like an empty nest or retirement can signal a time when troubles move in like swarming locusts on a grain field and strip your life of everything you care about.

That's certainly what the past four to six years have felt like for me. Like one loss after another, the trivial with the large, until I almost couldn't recognize the landscape of my life.

During this time my grandson Chad compared me to Job in the Bible. And while I am certainly no Job, I can understand a little of what he meant. Like Job, I had a wonderful life, a life I loved and was thankful for—and one I used to serve the Lord. Like Job, I suffered a series of painful blows and severe losses over a short period of time. Like Job, I learned a lot about myself and about God—and I witnessed his power and majesty more directly than I had ever seen before. And like Job as well, I am now enjoying a time of restoration, when things are getting better and I am enjoying something of the life I enjoyed before my cancer hit, although I am also aware I'll never really be the same again.

But let me hurry to add that in many ways I'm not like Job at all. My struggles have never been as cosmic or as dramatic. My friends and family have loved and supported me instead of questioning and arguing with me like Job's "comforters." And unlike Job, I never really felt the need to argue my case with God, never felt that my season of loss was unjust or inappropriate. "Why me" was never an issue for me. Rather, I always felt "Why not me."

I'm not sure exactly why this last is true. Perhaps it was simply a case of God's particular mercy that I was spared this kind of doubt. Bob thinks it has something to do with my gift of faith. But I think it's more because I know very well my locust years are nothing special—others have gone through much more than I have.

I know some of these people, or I have heard about them or read their stories. Some cancer patients, for instance, have been deserted by their spouses when they became sick or have been treated by incompetent or insensitive health professionals. Some people have been in accidents that paralyzed or disfigured them. Some have lost husbands and wives and children to death—pain I cannot begin to imagine—or faced violence and abuse. Some have been deserted by their spouses after years of lies; others have struggled for years to make ends meet.

When I think of the difficulties some of my fellow humans have endured, I can only be humbled. I am not Job. I am not a poster child for grief and loss or a symbol for anything. I certainly don't have it worse than anyone else.

And yet I do believe that locusts are locusts. When you are hurting, it doesn't really matter whether your loss is greater or less than someone else's loss—the hurt is still real. So perhaps some of the things I learned while living through my own locust season can be helpful to others who feel much of their lives is being stripped away.

So what have I learned? First of all, that the damage is real. I think it's important to recognize this to avoid the trap of being too glib or falsely sentimental. The losses we sustain during our stripping-down times are significant. The wounds inflicted are painful, and they usually leave scars. And while God has gifts to offer during our locust years, in this life, at least, they don't wipe out the painful memory of our losses. The riches of what we can learn and the bounty of God's continual provision can move us forward into more purposeful and abundant living. In fact, the "restored" life God often gives us to make up for lost locust years may be better in some ways than the life we had before—but it will never be the same.

I've always wondered how Job felt after his time of testing was over and God had restored everything he had lost. Once again he had children, cattle and sheep, servants, land, and possessions. Once again his wife and friends were supportive instead of critical. And yet children aren't inter-changeable. Memories of storms and fires and unsupportive friends aren't that easily set aside. Even for a man whose faith and trust won the approval of God himself, the knowledge of what he had gone through must have been painful.

The truth is that none of us ever gets through this world unmarked. All of us have troubles, all of us sustain losses we never completely get over. It's all part of living in a fallen world. Things happen. Things hurt us. Things we love are taken from us. And sometimes a "stripping season" will take us completely out of our old life and put us in a new, unfamiliar one. These seasons change us, and we can't ever be exactly the same person again.

The beauty of divine restoration, of course, is that God can and does use the very circumstances of our losses— even our locust-level losses—to teach us, strengthen us, and to give our lives new purpose and meaning. His gifts don't stop merely because our life changes, even when our life changes radically. His love doesn't let up merely because we're going through a bad patch or even a time of excruciating sorrow. His promise to redeem and restore our locust-eaten years holds true, even though we won't be completely restored or completely healed until we've finished with this life and gone on to glory. And even as we are in the midst of the devastation, watching the locusts fly in and rip apart our lives, he has already started on the process of teaching and renewing us.

This doesn't mean that God sends locusts into our lives to "teach us a lesson." I don't believe my cancer was a divine punishment for something I did or did not do. Although I do believe God disciplines his children, I don't think he normally inflicts catastrophes on us purely for educational purposes. He doesn't have to! This world produces quite enough pain, quite enough sin, to serve the Father as teaching tools. God doesn't need to manufacture more troubles just to bring us into line!

That said, I do believe God uses the locust years of our lives to special advantage. I believe he's done that for me. There's something about being stripped down to basics that has helped me get a better sense of who I am and who God is, of what is important and what is merely nice, of what I want and what God wants for me. Looking back, I can already see ways that God has worked through these insights and experiences to shape my character. And even now, as I see my life being restored—new house, new health, less pain, even the possibility of speaking again—I find I value the lessons from the locust years as much as I do the restorations. And the gifts he gave me in the middle of my loss are especially precious to me.

What are these gifts God has sent me in care of the locusts? One is a stronger *confidence* in what is eternal— what cannot be touched by catastrophe. Even when much is lost, much survives.

There's a little anonymous poem that is passed around a lot in cancer circles. It's posted on clinic bulletin boards and written in cards shared over the Internet. It even has several different versions, and I haven't a clue who wrote the original or even which version was the first. But I think it holds a lot of wisdom not only for cancer patients but for anyone going through locust years. Here's how it goes:

> *Cancer is so limited...*
> *It cannot cripple love.*
> *It cannot shatter hope.*
> *It cannot corrode faith.*
> *It cannot eat away peace.*
> *It cannot destroy confidence.*
> *It cannot kill friendship.*

It cannot shut out memories.
It cannot silence courage.
It cannot invade the soul.
It cannot steal eternal life.
It cannot quench the Spirit.
It cannot lessen the power of resurrection.

When you go through a thing like cancer, you realize how much truth that little poem holds. There's a catch to it, though. It is true that no external circumstances can invade the soul or quench the Spirit or lessen the power of resurrection. But something like cancer *can* shatter hope and corrode faith and eat away peace…if we let it. In other words, there's an element of choice involved. External circumstances cannot eat away our peace or destroy our friendships, but we can let our peace or our friendships be ruined when we are under pressure. I think that is true of all the lessons God wants to teach us in our stripping-down times. Even in our lowest moments, he grants us the dignity of choice. The lessons are there for us, but we must choose to learn.

Probably the strongest lesson of confidence I've been taught (and chosen to learn) during the locust years is that God is always there. We might not always understand what he is doing—indeed, as Job learned, so much of God is beyond our knowing, so awesome and magnificent that the only proper response is humble awe. Often we can see what he's been doing only in retrospect. But this sovereign God, as Job also learned, is always present in our times of testing, laying down the limits of what can be done to us and continuing to provide what we need the most even when we think it's all been taken away.

I find it interesting to note that not even Job lost *everything* in his locust years. Although his wife and his friends gave him bad advice, for instance, they did not leave him, and after initially faltering they gathered around and supported him. And I, too, have to admit that my losses during the cancer years, though painful, were limited. I lost my health, but I didn't lose my husband. I lost my speaking ministry, but I didn't lose all of my income, and I still had insurance. I lost my autonomy, but I didn't lose my faith. Looking back both on what I lost and what remained, I can see the Father's sustaining hand. Even when all I could see were locusts, God was already doing damage control.

So God was present in my time of loss, as in Job's, as sovereign Lord and guardian-protector. But I have a real advantage over Job in that I know God also as the incarnate Christ, the "man of sorrows" who redeemed us by becoming human, taking our most painful circumstances onto himself. He is very familiar with the experience of loss—first of his kingly nature to become a human baby, then of all his earthly possessions, finally of his life. And he suffered these losses willingly for our sake. When I was hurting, humiliated, and in pain, I had only to remember my Savior stripped naked, beaten, and crucified to know I was not alone. There is no cross he could ask me to bear that would equal his own. There is no promise of restoration more potent than the reality of his resurrection.

And there is no barren, locust-eating landscape I can walk through that isn't warmed and softened by the presence of God the Holy Spirit. I learned that as well during my locust years. He is the Comforter and Counselor who continued to guide and inspire and teach me. It was by the work of the Holy Spirit that I found my life producing fruit even in the midst of a locust-eaten field. Even when I was hurting, I could hear the Spirit's prompting to slip a note under a neighbor's door. When I was too weak to pray, I could feel the Spirit interceding "with groans that words cannot express" (see Romans 8:26).

So...God is present in my locust-eaten life, and my growing confidence in this reality is one of the gifts I've been given in my locust years.

Another gift has been the sometimes bittersweet gift of *humility.*

What is humility? Most of us think of it in terms of modesty, not bragging or boasting, not thinking too much of ourselves. We think of it in terms of bowing the head and submitting to authority. And there's an element of truth to all this, but I think there's more.

The great preacher Charles H. Spurgeon defined humility as "a right estimate of one's self," especially in comparison with God. I think of it as more the message of "Jesus Loves Me":

> *Little ones to Him belong,*
> *They are weak, but He is strong.*

When I fully recognize that simplest of facts, when I acknowledge both my weakness and God's strength and open myself to doing things his way, I am humbling myself as the Bible encourages us to do. I'm giving up my claim to power and control. And while I've never really considered myself proud or vain, I found during my illness that this kind of humility is harder for me than I thought.

One of the hardest losses for me to endure, you see, was the loss of my independence, my dignity, and my control over myself and my circumstances. As anyone who has experienced long-term medical treatment knows, being sick can be a profoundly humbling, even humiliating, experience—even under the best of circumstances. Being physically stripped, poked, prodded, even written on, goes hand in hand with the emotional and spiritual experience of being weak and helpless—and neither is easy for a person who has always cherished being in control. But the gift of such humbling, I learned, is that it brings us back down to a true recognition of who we are—mortal creatures with very little real control of our lives, but also children of a loving, caring God.

This is not to say we should give up all our pride. We need to hang on to a certain amount of personal dignity just to keep going. When Bob and I were in Seattle, for instance, I made a point of always getting up and getting dressed, even if all I wore were sweats. At night, I made a point of changing out of my day clothes. These simple acts of control and normality helped keep my spirits up and keep me from feeling like a total invalid.

And yet there were times when I had to simply give up all claim to pride and let others take care of me. It was in these moments that I felt most keenly my loss of control over the most basic of my body functions. The humiliation of such times can be hard to handle, especially for a person who has always preferred the power position of giving, not taking.

As a mother, for instance, I have been used to wiping up all manner of messes. But one of the humiliating realities of being seriously ill is that there are times when you're the one who makes messes and someone has to clean up after you. To realize that Bob and my friends and doctors and nurses have had to take care of me in this very intimate way has been a particularly difficult loss. And yet there was a gift in this loss as I experienced being tenderly cared for and made to feel comfortable. It's humbling, but it's also beautiful.

There was a particular time, in the hospital, when a nurse arrived in my room. There was a moment of silence as I realized, first, that it was time for my shower, and second, that the nurse assigned to me was a young man. He must have seen the doubt on my face, but he was kind and matter-of-fact. "Oh, dear Jesus," I prayed to myself, "I don't know if I can do this." But after days in bed I felt grubby and oily, and I knew I didn't have the strength to take a shower by myself. So I took a deep breath, walked in the little bathroom, and took my robe off. They had a little stool and shower curtain. "Don't leave me," I told the nurse, "because I can't do this by myself."

Talk about a humbling experience! This young man got in the shower with me and helped me stay on my feet. He saw to it that I washed my rear and under my arms. He kept the soap out of my eyes and made sure I was completely rinsed.

But here's the beauty that came with the humbling. Within seconds of entering that shower, all my trepidation had vanished. I didn't see that young nurse as male or female, but as an agent of the Lord's mercy. How I needed that shower, that sense of being clean and fresh! The nurse helped me dry off and put on a clean nightie. By the time we were through, I wanted to hug him. An experience I feared as a humiliation had turned into a tender gift of grace—because my need forced me into a position of trust and humility.

An even more vivid memory of such a time comes from a frightening incident when I actually went into a coma due to an infection. When Bob couldn't rouse me he called an ambulance and—well, there's no other way to put this—when he picked me up I lost all control of my bodily functions. Bob wiped me off the best he could, then handed me over to the ambulance drivers, saying he would meet me at the hospital. He stayed to face the unpleasant task of cleaning up that noxious mess. (What a star that man will have in heaven for that one.)

Meanwhile, I was whisked to the hospital and stabilized, and I finally began to come to just about the time the nurses came in to give me a bed bath. I remember how weak I felt, as helpless as a newborn. But they gently bathed me and powdered me and put me into a clean bed with a clean sheet over me. And again I felt myself dissolve in gratitude.

That, too, was a very humbling experience but a great lesson—to be grateful for God's mercies no matter what form they take. Humility, in fact, is one of the great lessons that a stripping time can teach. It was Job's great lesson. It is not an insignificant thing to learn just how weak we are, how strong God is, how desperately we need God and his love.

But once again, as with any of God's lessons, the lesson of humility is not automatic. Even when we're weak and beaten down, we still have choices between gratitude and submission or bitterness and rebellion. Our culture tends to glorify the rebellious response, to praise those who are "bloody but unbowed." And I met quite a few people in the cancer clinic who reacted furiously to their circumstances.

But in my experience, at least, the way of humility was the way to true restoration. Whenever, by the Lord's grace, I was able to choose the way of humility, I received the direct benefits of the Father's care, with the added benefit of then being more open to the Spirit's guidance.

I've come to believe, in fact, that *openness* is the key to almost all the gifts the Lord has to give us during our locust-years, to almost all the lessons he has to teach. If we let it, the experience of being stripped can open us up—opening our hearts and our minds and our spirits for something new.

Something about my experience with cancer, for instance, opened up my heart and my compassion and made me more sensitive to the losses of others.

Not that I wasn't compassionate before. Ever since I began my ministry, I've had a heart for the women who came to my seminars. I've loved them and wanted to help them. I also wanted to do my part to help others more directly—working in my church to organize a hospitality kitchen, for instance.

But while I always cared, I was never what you would call a tender or sympathetic person. This may surprise those who haven't known me well, but I've always been a very practical, direct, no-nonsense sort. My tendency when others had trouble was more to buck them up and urge them on. (That's the way I dealt with my own troubles as well.) When one of my children fell down and skinned a knee, I was more apt to help them up quickly, treat the boo-boo with a quick kiss and a Band-Aid, and send them on their way than to coddle and comfort them.

There was nothing really wrong with the way I was. My children knew I loved them, and people I ministered to felt my care and compassion. But something has changed in me since the locusts flew into my life. Something has softened in me. My heart is far more open, more tender, more aware of the hurt in others. Not only do I want to help people who struggle; I am moved to weep with them. I really believe that God has worked in my time of loss to make me a more loving, vulnerable, compassionate woman. My heart feels bigger. In a sense my _world_ feels bigger.

And if my locust years have worked to give me a more open heart, they have given me more open hands as well. I tend to hold everything with a little looser grasp. And this is quite a change for me.

I am by nature a collector, a nester, a settler—not a pilgrim. As a woman who grew up poor, I have always gotten a lot of pleasure in gathering my "stuff" around me. As a woman who grew up in a broken family, I love to gather all my chicks under my wing. I like building on a foundation more than starting something new. Like most of us, I'm not wild about change.

But I've come to believe there are times in our lives when we are called to leave one thing behind and move on to another, and going through a time of loss can also teach us how to do this. Sometimes it takes a time of loss for us to loosen our stranglehold grip on the familiar and give us the freedom we need to step forward into a new future.

A friend of mine once told me that she had never voluntarily left a nest (meaning a position or circumstance). She always had to be kicked out, but usually when she was kicked out it was time to go. I believe that my particular time of loss has helped do that to me. As much as I loved— and still love—my ministry, my house, my life, I think perhaps it was time to move on. At very least, it was time to back off, to travel less, perhaps to rethink the direction of our ministry, and in this sense my season of loss may well have served a positive purpose in our lives. I cannot say with any certainty whether this is true. I can say, however, that after my season of loss I find myself with a different view of my nest. I still love my "stuff," but I'm not quite so firmly attached to it. I still love my family, but I am more willing to let them live their own lives.

And I've also learned to let go a little of another of my prized possessions, my looks. Actually, it was a surprise to realize how much I depended on being attractive. I never really thought of myself as vain, but I see in retrospect that looking good to others was something I depended on from childhood.

For women, especially, looks are a form of power, and I was accustomed to wielding that power. Even as a small child, I knew I had the power to charm my daddy. As an older child, though I was very shy, I always dressed well, thanks to my mother's skill with a sewing machine and her connections in the clothing industry. As a young adult and then later as a professional speaker, my looks also served me. I've never been Hollywood-gorgeous, but I cleaned up well, and that helped give me confidence. And I always knew Bob appreciated my efforts to stay fit and lovely for him.

So even though I wasn't exactly vain, the changes my cancer and its treatment brought about challenged me more than I ever expected. I really felt the loss of my physical attractiveness.

My initial thinness didn't really bother me that much because at first I thought it resulted from my healthy diet—and besides, thin is always "in" in Southern California. The loss of my hair was not a major blow—though it is to many—because I expected it to grow back quickly. I had fun finding pretty scarves and hats to cover my bald head. And even when my hair grew back gray I got a cute short haircut and accepted the compliments from people who thought it looked great.

But as my cancer progressed, my discomfort with my looks grew. Losing my hair a second and a third time was more of a blow. Having my body grow soft and lumpy—though still thin—from lack of exercise was a blow. Then, after the bone marrow transplant, I reached the point where I would look in the mirror and not recognize myself. My face was round and puffy from antirejection drugs and red and shiny from graft-versus-host disease. My eyes squinted above chipmunk cheeks. My body was swollen, too, and lumpy under my "cancer uniform" of sweatpants and sweatshirt. With my gray hair and shuffling gait I looked like an old lady—but a puffy, red-faced, squinty-eyed old lady. And I hated looking that way. When old friends would visit, I felt I needed to warn them ahead of time so I wouldn't have to see the shock on their faces.

I knew, of course, that the way I looked was a pretty trivial issue. I knew being alive was much more important than being beautiful. And yet this was an issue I really struggled with. I just had a hard time not looking like *me*.

Today, the situation is a little better. I have been able to taper off various medications and shake off the graft-versus-host disease, and the puffiness has gone down. As I have gained strength and begun to exercise again, my body is feeling a little more streamlined. And as for my chic cap of gray hair that grew in after chemotherapy—well, I went to the beauty salon as soon as the doctor said it was okay, and now my hair is magically dark again! My grandson Chad told me just the other day, "Grammy, you're looking more like your picture!"

I thank God for this restoration of my looks. But now I'm discovering that the experience of becoming a pudgy, squinting, shuffling old lady really did change something deep inside me. I'll probably always care about how I look—because of my upbringing and because of my profession and because I'm such a visual person. And yet now, looking back, I realize I really have let go of a lot of worry over appearances. In fact, I believe I'll be able to withstand the natural changes of growing older with more serenity now that I've realized I can be loved no matter what I look like.

Looking back at my early life, I can see that I grew up thinking only my mother loved me. Everyone else had conditions. My aunt, for instance, would slip me $50 on the condition that I would come visit and call her often.

"You be a good little girl," she would say, "and one day you'll get my diamond ring." Other relatives would comment on what a "pretty little girl" I was, and I got the message early that being pretty and little was another condition for being loved and accepted.

In light of that background, it has been a revelation to me to realize just how deep and unconditionally I am loved—and how little my looks have to do with it. My relationship with Bob, for instance, has only grown deeper and warmer over the course of this illness, and my gray hair and fat cheeks and lumpy body have been very much beside the point. My children and my grandchildren and my friends didn't care what I looked like; they just wanted me well. My fellow patients at Dr. Barth's office and the Hutch never knew me any other way, and they loved me just as they found me. And God, of course, is far more concerned with the beauty of my spirit than with any part of me on the outside.

I've always known that beauty is only skin deep. But in the cancer clinics, where so many of us are less than lovely, you really do get a sense of who is truly beautiful. For it is in the context of bald heads and lopsided chests and laser-burned skin and surgical incisions you realize how gorgeous a godly spirit and a positive attitude can be.

Because coping with my changing appearance was more of a struggle than I ever anticipated, I was deeply moved to read the words of a fellow cancer sufferer named Terry Healey. This poor man had to go through so much more than I did. Because of facial tumors, he had to undergo massively disfiguring facial surgery while still in his early 20s—losing half his nose, half his lip, the bones on one side of his face. Plastic surgery could only make him what they called "streetable." But Terry Healey went on to marry and live a useful life ministering to other cancer victims. "We all struggle with insecurities in one form or another," he wrote. "For me it took something extremely devastating—something that would take me to the deepest depths of self-evaluation—to realize that battle scars are what makes someone interesting; battle scars are what makes someone wise; battle scars are what makes you realize how precious and valuable life really is; battle scars are what prepare you for the inevitable adversity that lies ahead."[1]

That kind of perspective shift is yet another gift that locust years can bring you. In addition to opening your spirit with humility and opening your heart with compassion and opening your hands to loosen your grip, a stripping-down time can open your eyes to the true wonder and beauty that fills every day, even the most ordinary.

Looking back, I don't know if I really appreciated all the years of health and vigor the Lord had given me. Did I truly understand the gift of physical strength and energy? Did I truly comprehend how beautiful the world is, how blue the sky can be, how precious is every human being I meet?

There are times even now, as I'm doing better, when I see someone my age who is vibrant, has vigor, and is walking or jogging or riding a bike. I wonder if they appreciate the beauty all around them, the sheer enjoyment of just doing activities. I do know now, as I seem to be on the mend, that my eyes are wide open and I appreciate everything so much more. Each moment has a sparkle. With each person or activity, I think "I may never see that again."

We took a trip to New England this past autumn and stayed in a lovely little inn in Freeport, Maine. I found myself reveling in the snowy tablecloths and napkins, the beautiful breakfast buffet, and the warmer-than-usual wind. We took a drive in the country, and I was almost overwhelmed by the Indian-summer blueness, the iridescent leaves that feathered down onto the still-green meadows. Then we crossed a bridge over a gorge, stopping to look down into the faraway water.

I know it's a cliché, but it's an honest one. As I sat looking out over that beautiful scene—and with my shingles pain still burning, I thought, "If my life never gets better than this, we will be all right." My awareness of what I had lost—and how quickly I had lost it—made my appreciation of what I now had so much more intense.

No, I am not the woman I was four years ago. And though in wistful moments I find myself missing her— missing my old life—I know I would never want to go back. For in these years—these locust years, these stripping-down years—I have gained as much as I lost.

Yes, I lost my health and my looks. But I gained a firmer sense of who I am (anyway) and who God is. I have become closer to the Lord, felt his presence, felt his arms around me, I have felt his words of comfort in my heart, and I have felt his voice saying, "Emilie, I'm not through with you yet. Together we can stand, and together we can share what I've done in your life."

Yes, I lost my speaking ministry and much of our business. But I gained a firmer sense of trust that what God wants to happen in our life, he'll make happen. (And we're already getting offers for me to speak in the future.) I also gained a new sense of mission to women who are hurting— I can't wait to bring God's message of mercy and his compassion to others who know pain.

Yes, I lost my sense of control over my own body. But I also gained in the sweet humility that comes with acknowledging my own weakness and receiving help from others the tender sense of being cared for.

Yes, I lost a degree of freedom and autonomy to do what I please. But I gained a new appreciation of what such small

102 A DIFFERENT KIND OF MIRACLE

pleasures can mean, so that now I truly relish a walk around the block.

Yes, I lost the innocence of a pain-free existence, but I gained a deep new compassion for those who hurt—and a new realization that I want to serve the Lord even more than I want to live without pain. I also found a kind of wisdom that comes from learning to be patient and learning to take comfort from the Lord. I even received a beautiful card from a man whose daughter is marrying without his blessing. He wrote, "Oh, that we could be wise without experiencing pain." And I thought, "Well, sometimes I could use a little less wisdom." But I also knew that he was right, and I found myself thanking God—yes, for the pain of my shingles.

I lost a lot of my energy and vitality. I gained a new appreciation for God's everyday gifts of strength. I gained a new knowledge that no matter what happens I am still me, and that I am loved whether I'm contributing or not.

Yes, I lost a lot. But I gained a renewed gratitude for what I kept—my family, my faith—and a stronger sense of what cannot be taken away from me. And then, on top of it all, I am in the process of being restored.

This is the wonderful gift the Lord can give us above all the gifts from the locust years. It's not guaranteed on this side of death, but it often happens. It happened to Job, and it is happening to me. Today, Bob and I truly have a sense that God is restoring the years the locusts have eaten.

In 2001, for the first time in four years, Bob and I hosted a Christmas tea in our home. New neighbors and old friends alike were invited—and we made a special attempt to reach out to people who might need to know Christ. We served our traditional waffles with a few new dishes added. And then, as we have done so often before, we lit candles and asked each guest to share a special Christmas memory or thought.

Tears ran down my face that night as I looked around that lovely candlelit room at faces both new and familiar. So much had changed for us in the past few years. So much had been lost. And yet I was surely seeing a fulfillment of the Lord's faithfulness.

There is no guarantee, of course, that there won't be other stripping seasons. It's almost a certainty, in fact, that seasons of loss are still in our future. Bob and I will grow older, so we will face the inevitable losses that come with aging. Something could still happen to our loved ones, and unless we die together in an accident, one of us will inevitably live with the loss of the other. And we will both face death, the ultimate stripping experience here on this earth.

But even then, we have the promise of restoration—and this will be one without scars. We will be the grateful recipients of a new "incorruptible" body and everlasting life with our Redeemer.

I don't know about you, but I can't wait for that final, beautiful gift.

MY DEAR FRIEND,

Are you at one of those points in life where you feel flattened, devastated, overwhelmed by grief and loss? It might not feel very comforting right now to be told that you're a prime candidate for the Lord's restoration. But you are.

Whether your losses are little or large, they are real and important. It's all right to mourn the years the locusts are eating in your life—even as you trust God to preserve the essentials and restore the beauty and abundance in your life. Remember, love is a prerequisite for grief. If you didn't love, you wouldn't really suffer from loss. So your suffering in a time of loss is really evidence of your love, and love is always a good thing.

In the meantime, if you haven't already begun to see God's purposes at work in your stripping-down time, you might want to consider: Is there something the Lord has for me to learn in this? About humility? About compassion? About appreciation? About letting go?

I urge you to consciously open yourself to his work. Humble yourself to learn. Open your heart to others. Open your eyes. Open your hands to release whatever it is you're gripping too tightly. Let the locusts have the bitterness and the resentment; you can't afford the negative energy. Focus instead on hope and possibilities.

And remember, no matter what is given and taken away, the Lord is still in control. God the Father, God the Son, and God the Holy Spirit will be with you always, providing for you, suffering with you, guiding you in the ways of peace.

God's richest blessings on you,

Emilie

GOD'S GIFT OF TRUTH
FOR YOUR LOCUST YEARS

⸕ God does some of his best work during times of loss.

⸕ Locust years can teach you humility, compassion, and appreciation if you let them. But their most powerful lesson may be how to let go and move on.

⸕ The man of sorrows, who lost everything for our sakes, walks with you through your times of pain and loss.

⸕ It's impossible to get through life without scars. But restoration is a true promise.

CHAPTER FIVE

Living in His Presence

O LORD, *I call to you; come quickly to me. Hear my voice when I call to you. May my prayer be set before you like incense; may the lifting up of my hands be like the evening sacrifice....My eyes are fixed on you, O Sovereign* LORD; *in you I take refuge—do not give me over to death.*

—PSALM 141:1-2,8

But thou, when thou prayest, enter into thy closet, and when thou hast shut thy door, pray to thy Father which is in secret; and thy Father which seeth in secret shall reward thee openly.

—MATTHEW 6:6 KJV

Do not be anxious about anything, but in everything, by prayer and petition, with thanksgiving, present your requests to God. And the peace of God, which transcends all understanding, will guard your hearts and your minds in Christ Jesus.

—PHILIPPIANS 4:6-7

5

LIVING IN HIS PRESENCE

Fifteen minutes with God...and how they grew

_c₃

For years, I've cherished the time I spent in my "prayer closet."

But I never thought I'd actually be praying *in* my closet.

It started a little before my April birthday, almost a year after my bone marrow transplant. Bob and I were living in Newport Beach, and we were scheduled for an appointment with Dr. Barth the next morning.

"Honey, I want to take you shopping for some new clothes," Bob told me. "You've been kind of living in your cancer clothes, and I think something new would lift your spirits."

Well, he was right. For three years I had worn little but my slouchy, comfortable sweats. But to be honest, new clothes were the furthest thing from my mind. That was a time when my shingles pain was a constant torment, and all I wanted was for my clothes to be loose and comfortable. I didn't really feel much like shopping, either.

Still, it was sweet of Bob to be concerned. So we decided to go out after my appointment the next day, first to a late breakfast and then to Fashion Island, our local mall, for a little shopping.

Before we ever got to Fashion Island, though, I'd seen something else I wanted a lot more.

I found it in the rest room, of all places. The restaurant where we went for breakfast is a cute little establishment, sort of a combination antique shop and restaurant, and most of the décor is for sale. While Bob and I waited for our food, I made a quick pit stop, and there in the rest room I saw the most enchanting little chair. It had short legs and leaned back just a bit. When I saw it, my spirit immediately announced that it would make the most perfect prayer chair.

I actually called Bob into the bathroom to see it. I told him I would really like a chair like that instead of clothes I'd eventually give away. Red-faced from being taken into the ladies room, he just smiled and agreed with me that it was a cute little chair.

Well, a few days later I woke up and padded over to our big walk-in closet to fetch some comfy sweats. I turned on the light, and then I started screaming, "Oh my gosh!"

There in the closet was that precious little chair from the restaurant. Resting beside it was my heart-shaped prayer basket with my Bible and my prayer notebook. And on the chair was a note in Bob's handwriting: "Happy birthday to my wonderful wife."

I couldn't stop crying. *He still loves me*, I thought. *Even with my fat face and my chubby cheeks and my out-of-shape body and gray hair and sores in my mouth, he loves me. He's had to care for me, clean up after me, give me pills and injections, and still he loves me and thinks I'm a wonderful wife.*

I think you can understand why I love that little chair in my closet! But actually, there's more to the story.

You see, prayer really has been important to me for many years. Ever since I gave my life to Christ at age 15, I have desired to spend regular time with the Lord, and over the years I have devised ways to make prayer time a regular part of my days. As a busy young mom, I learned that prayer and a quiet time could easily be crowded out of my schedule, so I devised some practical strategies to help me overcome these problems.

First, because my life was so full and fragmented, I decided I was more likely to be faithful in small increments, so I concentrated on setting aside just 15 minutes a day to spend alone with God. I also discovered that settling down to prayer was easier when I kept all my devotional tools together in a little basket that could be carried anywhere and actually wrote down what I wanted to pray about in a little notebook.

Over the years, my prayer basket and prayer notebook kept my prayer life on track. Seeing my little basket beside a chair would remind me to pick it up and go somewhere to spend time with the Lord. My prayer notebook would remind me of people I'd promised to pray for, issues I needed to pray for, prayers I had already prayed. My Bible and sometimes an inspirational book would help me focus my thoughts and turn my heart toward the Lord. I always kept a box of tissues in the basket because praying sometimes moved me to tears, and I also kept notecards, a pen, and stamps there in case I was moved to write a note of sympathy or encouragement. Sometimes I kept a spray of silk flowers to remind me of the fragrance of God's love. Sometimes I would tuck in another little keepsake, such as a picture one of the grandchildren drew or a loving note from a friend.

Year after year, as I used the tools in my prayer basket, I felt my faith increase. I felt my joy in my Father's presence grow as I spent regular time with him. As my children grew and my life changed, my 15 minutes with God would sometimes stretch out a little. Sometimes I would spend half an hour at a time—or even longer on a few occasions.

Then came our Jenny's divorce, which seemed to wrench our family apart. How I worried over my daughter, who seemed to have thrown aside her faith and everything else important. How I ached for her three children, trying to cope with a broken home and a mother who was so caught up in her own needs she couldn't face their hurt. How I worried over Bob, who was so furious with Jenny he could barely speak. And how I struggled with my own conflicting feelings of anger, shame, and love.

Suddenly, I found that 15 minutes of prayer a day—even a "long 15 minutes"—just wasn't enough. That's when I began using my daily exercise walks as additional prayer time. And here again, I found a tool that helped me focus my prayers. I used a little book by Lee Roberts called *Praying God's Will for My Daughter*, a collection of Scriptures shaped into prayer form. Each day for at least 45 minutes, as I walked the irrigation canal near our home, I would use those Scripture prayers as prompts as I brought my concerns to the Lord. Weeks turned into months, seasons, and years as I prayed through that book. Then I went back to the beginning and started again.

What was happening, of course, was that my habit of spending regular time with God in ordinary times was driving me to spend *more* time with him in a time of acute need. Although I had always believed prayer was important, I was learning something about prayer in time of trouble, which is that in times of difficulty you tend to do more of what you're already doing.

Think about it. If you're a drinker, what do you do in times of high stress, high worry, high fear? What you do is drink more.

If worry and anxiety send you straight to the refrigerator, where are you apt to go in a crisis?

Because I was in the habit of turning to the Lord on a regular basis, bringing him my concerns and trying to listen for his voice, in times of difficulty I found myself hungrier than ever for time with him. And so my 15 minutes grew during those worrisome years into an hour or more.

But those prayer times on the canal were so much more than intercession over Jenny's life. They were also preparing me for my future time of need, preparing me for a different kind of prayer that would carry me through my illness.

You see, when cancer struck our household—and make no mistake, cancer strikes whole families, not just individuals—my first instinct was to run to my heavenly Father. Bob ran, too. From the very beginning of our long and confusing journey, the prayers from our house were fervent and continual.

Dr. Larry Keefauver, in his wonderful book *When God Doesn't Heal Now*, provides a helpful list of ways for a Christian to pray. He urges us to:

- pray humbly
- pray boldly, persisting in faith
- pray continually
- pray in faith for your need
- pray for others
- pray with praise
- pray in his name and will

♭ pray to receive

♭ pray with another in agreement

♭ pray the Word[2]

Well, we prayed all those ways, and probably added a few approaches to the list. We prayed for guidance—in choosing a doctor, in moving to a new city, in disposing of our business, in making decisions about treatment. We prayed for strength—for both of us in coping with unsettling changes in our lives, for me in enduring the uncomfortable side effects of the treatments, for Bob in managing the significant workload that comes with being a caregiver. We prayed for our children and grandchildren and all the people in our lives who worried about us and loved us. As we met more and more fellow cancer patients, we prayed for them. We prayed for my healing, of course. We prayed again and again, posting petition after petition on the doors of heaven.

Whenever we could, we gathered with fellow believers and joined our hearts for sweet times of prayer. Almost every visit eventually turned into a prayer circle, as people who cared for us held our hands and entered with us into the presence of God. Twice we followed the advice found in the fifth chapter of James and gathered the elders of the church, who prayed for my healing and anointed me with oil—a truly beautiful, moving experience.

But there was another kind of praying I began to do more and more by myself, especially in those dark hours of the night when I would wake and hurt and worry. More and more I began to just *be* with the Lord, sharing my fear with him, telling him how I felt. In my heart I was cuddling up to my heavenly Daddy, leaning on him and laying my head on his shoulder. In the daytime, too, when I would be lying on the couch, too worn out and in too much pain to move, my eyes unable to focus, my mouth too sore to speak, I would simply rest in the Lord, letting myself be aware of his presence, depending on him to carry me through.

What I was learning in those very difficult days was that pain can bring you closer to God. Not because pain is a good thing in itself, but because it gives you a stronger incentive to seek out God and his grace. There's a certain level of pain, I found, where your only choice is either to lean on God's grace moment by moment or to just jump out the window and die. I chose to lean, and I found God's grace truly is sufficient. I experienced that grace in his loving presence. I experienced it as almost a physical sensation, right there beside my pain. I truly believe God has used the circumstance of my pain to draw me closer and closer to him—though admittedly there were times when I wondered how close I had to get.

I even reached the point in my prayer time that I sincerely thanked God for my bout with shingles, because without it I never would have been able to experience to the extent of his faithfulness a love that was strong enough to carry me even through the most agonizing pain I had ever felt. (After I thanked him, though, I asked him politely once more if he could take it away.)

By that time, of course, even 15 minutes a day in prayer were far behind me. Often, because of my medication, I couldn't manage a formal devotional time anyway. I rarely had the energy or the mental focus to read devotional books or write in my prayer journal, and the only Bible readings I could manage were found in the verses Bob read aloud to me and the gentle Christian music we played.

But still those were sweet times, those long hours spent in the Lord's presence while my body and my medical regiment battled those renegade cancer cells. And I'm not sure I would have known how to find him if it hadn't been for all those 15 minutes with my prayer basket, all those hours on the canal path. If I hadn't learned to trust God in praying for Jenny, I wonder if I would have rested in him quite so easily when I was so sick. If I hadn't experienced firsthand both his faithfulness and his mysterious ways of working, I wonder if I could have kept on trusting him when the healing we prayed for seemed all but impossible.

I will admit, however, that there were days in my long cancer journey when even quiet communion with God seemed almost beyond me. I was weak, in constant pain, discouraged that none of my treatments seemed to be working, and frustrated when every doctor's visit was followed by another one. I was sick of waiting rooms, sick of couches, sick of sickness. And Bob, too, reached times of discouragement when praying seemed like too much effort.

Those were the times when we would look at all the cards and letters sent in by people who promised to pray for me. Often I couldn't even read them because my eyes wouldn't focus right. But I knew each card represented a prayer. So I would pick them up one by one and imagine those prayers rising around me like incense to my heavenly Father. And I would no longer be hanging. I would be lifted up, buoyed by all those beautiful prayers.

When I was a child, I loved to play on the monkey bars at the playground. I loved to swing my little body from bar to bar and clamber to the top. (Oh, to have that kind of strength and energy again!) But once in a while I would get myself into an awkward position where I was hanging by my hands by a bar—a little too high to jump down, and not quite able to pull myself up or get a leg over the bar. I still remember that panicky feeling: "Help me, help me, I'm going to fall!" And then someone would come over and give me a boost. And I wouldn't fall.

That's what the prayers of others felt like to me during the toughest times of my cancer treatment. They were a boost that kept me from falling. I'll never forget that sense of being lifted when I had no lift left in me. That alone is enough to make me believe passionately in the power of prayer.

But that's not to say that prayer was a simple matter in my cancer experience. I think that prayer almost always raises some questions in times of trouble because what we pray and the way the Lord answers are sometimes quite different.

What we saw and experienced in the hospital and cancer clinics was enough to occasionally shake up our ideas about prayer. The truth is, an extreme circumstance like cancer tends to bring a person face-to-face both with the power of prayer and the problems of prayer. Bob and I became acutely aware during our cancer years that prayer is not the simple transaction some make it out to be.

There were times when we had the amazing experience of seeing immediate, positive "results" from our prayers, for instance, when a focused campaign of intercessory prayer dramatically changed my white blood count over a period of days. Just as often, though, we would pray for one thing and something else would happen. Or prayers would often be answered with a no or a not yet. Or sometimes, it seems, with dead silence.

I had several friends who took it on themselves to focus their prayers specifically on my shingles pain. Month after month, year after year, they added their petitions to mine, asking for relief to hasten my healing. And month after month, year after year, I was tortured by that burning and stabbing on my torso. It was only after two years of suffering that I found any relief at all—through a specialist who offered me powerful narcotics. And only now, as my transplanted immune system takes hold, are those agonizing symptoms beginning to subside a little.

I have felt from the beginning that God was in the process of answering all those petitions for my relief. I know that I was healed long ago of the actual shingles, that the postherpetic pain was just a lingering effect, and that it would probably diminish as I grew stronger. But I have no answer for why this particular affliction seemed to resist so many fervent and specific prayers.

This happens in ordinary life, too, of course, but the stakes are so much higher in a crisis. And so the questions can be more poignant, more heartfelt. Why does God want us to pray for specific things, we wonder, if he's going to do what he wants to anyway? Should we just pray for God's will to be done and leave it at that? But if that's true, why does the Bible tell us to make our requests known to God? Does it make a difference to just make our requests and then tack on "If it be thy will"?

These are classic theological dilemmas, of course. And Bob was probably more bothered by such questions than I was. Perhaps it's because he has a more analytical, questioning mind than I do. Perhaps it was because he was healthy and felt the frustration of waiting more than I did. He says that there were times we prayed the same prayers so often that he actually got bored with saying them. He wondered if we should just assign numbers to them and save time: "Lord we pray that you would take care of number three, and number 11 is really on our hearts today." He was half kidding, of course, but I know his understanding of prayer was challenged quite a bit during these years. And I think a lot of people feel the same at one time or another.

The hard truth is that God's ways are not our ways; his timing is not our timing. Though he answers prayer, his answers and his method of answering are not always what we would choose. God's ways are mysterious, and this can be intensely frustrating, especially when we're feeling weak or frightened and our life seems out of control. Every now and then we have to wait a long time to see our prayers answered, and this can be frustrating as well. And sometimes, when we seek the Lord's face, for one reason or another we have a hard time feeling his presence.

What Bob and I had to learn to do during these times of discouragement was pray specifically for faith and endurance. We prayed for signs that God was still at work in our lives, for discernment about our prayer questions. And we found that sooner or later, as we prayed this way, we would have a glimpse of light that kept us going.

One of the things that helped us most with the frustrations of prayer was the fact that we had been praying people before, and we began seeing the fulfillment of our *earlier* prayers right in the middle of our frustrating prayers about cancer.

On the very day that my ulcer struck with such agony, for instance, I had the beautiful experience of having my daughter pray for me. This was a woman who, to my knowledge, had never prayed out loud. She had never prayed for me. But now, in the most painful circumstances of my life, when we still didn't have any satisfactory answers about what was wrong with me, I was seeing the fruit of those years of praying for Jenny to grow and mature in the Lord.

And Jenny's story kept on unfolding in beautiful counterpoint to the progress of my illness, encouraging us always about the power of prayer. Even as I grew sicker and sicker, as various therapies didn't work, as our prayers for healing seemed to go unanswered, I found hope in seeing my prayers for Jenny's growth bear such beautiful fruit. For the first time, I saw her holding daily devotions with her family. I saw her using wisdom and restraint as she got to know her Bill, seeking the Lord's guidance and extensive counseling before she made a final decision. I saw her and Bill united in marriage, pledging to love and honor each other before the Lord. And wonder of wonders, I even saw Jenny and her former husband, Craig, after so much bitterness and pain, gradually forge a friendship and parental partnership—to the point that both of them with their new spouses have gone to dinner together and even played golf together.

On all the days I walked the canal path in Riverside, praying God's Word over my daughter and asking for a miracle of reconciliation between her and Craig, this was not the miracle I expected or wanted. And yet when I see the beauty God has forged out of a truly ugly situation, I am amazed at his wisdom, his power, his sheer inventiveness. Watching God's different kind of miracle unfold in Jenny's life, his better-than-I-asked-for answer to my prayers, was just the kind of encouragement Bob and I needed while we waited for answers to our prayers for healing.

What both of us learned in that experience of prayers answered while awaiting other answers is that prayer is an ongoing process—or, more accurately, part of an ongoing relationship. And like any relationship involving human beings, it has its ups and downs. In the prayer life of any given individual, there may be times of healthy communication and times of misunderstanding. There may be times of warm communion and times of chilly estrangement, of deep intimacy or stiff formality.

Unlike a human relationship, of course, the problems with prayer tend to be one-sided. We're usually the ones who misunderstand, who draw away, who forget to listen or who just can't hear because of our human limitations. We're the ones who fall into the trap of treating a loving relationship like a business transaction—"I do the praying. You do the answering." We're the ones who have difficulty setting aside 15 minutes a day to spend with the One who knows us best and loves us most.

In fact, perhaps the most amazing miracle of all is that God doesn't give up on us. He doesn't stop listening, doesn't stop caring, doesn't stop answering prayer. I've discovered, in fact, that he'll accept our prayers whenever and however we manage to bring them, and he can use even the most hesitant, awkward prayer as a creative tool for our ongoing redemption.

If we only throw him occasional "flash prayers" or only turn to him when we need something, he'll hear our prayers and take us from there.

If we can only manage 15 minutes a day, he'll honor our faithfulness in those 15 minutes and use that time to draw us closer to him.

If we need a gimmick or a tool to focus our minds and discipline our prayers, he'll bless us abundantly through that.

It only follows, though, that the more time we spend with him, the better we will get to know him, and the more freely his love will flow through our lives.

And that's where my brand-new prayer chair and my closet comes in.

The more I lived through in my season of illness, you see, the more I came to understand what a miracle prayer can be, and the more I desired a more profound relationship with the Lord. I wanted more of the Lord who had cared for me so tenderly and inventively.

My illness had already given me the gift of more time to spend in prayer.

Now, I discovered, I wanted a special place where I could go to spend time with him in solitude.

Actually, the reason I thought "prayer" when I saw that cute little chair in the restaurant bathroom was a wonderful thing my friend Donna Otto had done when she remodeled her home. She built a special little room at the end of a walk-in closet, behind a push-out mirror. In that lovely little secret space, she placed a wingback chair, an antique kneeling stool, and some shelves with devotional books. She could go into that "prayer closet," close the door, and no one would know she was even in the house.

I just loved that room when Donna showed it to me. *How heavenly,* I thought, *to have that privacy, that uninterrupted time with the Lord.* So when we moved into our new house in Newport Beach, I started looking for something that could serve as a prayer closet for me. I noted our large bedroom closet has louvered doors and the lighting in there is good. All I needed was a place to sit, and Bob's loving birthday present gave me that.

So now when I have my prayer time, I really do go in my closet. I sit in my low-slung prayer chair with my prayer basket beside me. It still holds my prayer notebook and my Bible and a devotional book and Kleenex and pen and cards—plus a new pair of "cheater glasses" and a little beanbag "prayer bear" with its hands folded.

And it's when I'm there in my closet, settling down for time with the God who has given me so much, that I realize how far I've traveled when it comes to prayer.

When I was younger, people used to say to me, "Oh, you know I pray at least an hour a day." I would hear people say, "The less time I have, the more time I need to spend with God." And while I really admired these marathon pray-ers, I just couldn't imagine myself doing it. I wanted to be faithful, and I believed in prayer. But to be honest, I couldn't even think of anything that would take me an hour to pray about. I couldn't imagine sitting still for so long.

Well, I've changed. I've reached the point in my life where I can literally spend hours in my prayer chair, and sometimes I do. Occasionally Bob has to knock on the louvered doors and make sure I'm all right.

What do I do while I'm there? I usually start by binding the enemy from me, my family, and my house. I cleanse my heart with the Lord and ask that above all, his will might be done. I read some Scripture. I leaf through my prayer notebook, lifting up others to the Lord and bringing him my personal requests as well. I pray for continued healing, for easing of the shingles pain. Then I just sit and meditate, letting God speak to me in the stillness. Sometimes I'll write down impressions I have. Sometimes I'll have an impression that I need to write someone a note or lift up a particular issue to the Lord. Sometimes I weep for my friends and acquaintances who are struggling with cancer or other hard circumstances. Sometimes I just lean my head on the Lord's shoulder the way I learned to do in the midnight hours when I was sick.

It has been a wonderful blessing, this prayer chair, and I consider it a gift both from my Bob and from the Lord. From Bob, it was a confirmation of his ongoing love. From the Lord, it was a dispensation of peace, the quiet center I had longed for, a chance to get to know him better and better.

I consider my deepened prayer life, in fact, as one of the most profound gifts the Lord had for me in my cancer experience. When I turned to him in my time of deepest need, God's arms felt as real and familiar to me as Bob's hand in mine. When I was confused, I heard his voice of guidance in my ears. I felt his balm on my spirit even as my nerve endings burned with pain. I walked with his strength, slept under his watch, and knew his presence in the most sterile hospital ward. There were times when I could almost see him at work in my very cells, and I still crave that closeness for my life.

In my times of deepest weakness, as well, I felt the power of other people's intercession, so I understood more deeply than ever the fellowship of prayer that unites the body of Christ. I love to pray the Lord's Prayer now because I imagine so many other Christians around the world, praying Jesus' words along with me in hundreds of different languages and confessing a hundred variations of "debts" and "trespasses." And because I have known what it is to be lifted up by praying friends, I am moved much more strongly to pray for others.

For me, these days, prayer is not just a duty, not just a "good thing." It is so much more than a "should." It's a literal lifeline, and it's also a sacred privilege, an opportunity for one-on-one time with the Creator of the universe, the Redeemer of my soul, the Healer of my body, the Source of all love.

That's ample reason, I'd say, for all that time I'm spending in my closet these days.

MY DEAR FRIEND,

If you are going through a difficult time, you need prayer more than you need answers, more than you need medicine, more than you need friends or money or wisdom. No matter what your current circumstances, you need as much time in the presence of your heavenly Father as you can get.

But if the idea of spending hours in prayer boggles your mind, don't worry. In prayer, as in other aspects of the spiritual life, God will take you where you are and grow you from there. Here are some ideas that might help you spend more meaningful time in his presence.

- ♭ To build your faith in prayer, write down specific prayer petitions and leave a space to write down the answers you receive. You'd be surprised how easy it is to forget what the Lord has done!

- ♭ When prayer doesn't come easily, try priming the pump with words of Scripture or prayers others have written. If prayer still eludes you, just try to "lean your heart" toward God and let the Holy Spirit speak for you.

- ♭ Claim the healing or resolution that God is working in your life—even when you can't see anything happening. God is faithful. You can trust him to bring you the best in due time.

- ♭ Ask everyone you know for prayer—and specifically ask a few real "prayer warriors" to hold you up. When times are tough and you're barely hanging on, concentrate on the mental image of these brothers and sisters praying for you.

- ♭ Ask God for what you need and what you desire— but be willing to accept the fact that God may answer in a way, and on a timetable, you never expected. If you have difficulties with prayer or questions about how it works, don't hesitate to bring those to the Lord as well.

♭ Whenever possible, keep up the discipline of a prayer routine, even if it's only 15 minutes—or five minutes—a day. Don't hesitate to use gimmicks and reminders, even corny ones, to remind you and keep you on track.

If you do these things, "the peace of God, which transcends all understanding, will guard your hearts and your minds in Christ Jesus" (Philippians 4:7). What else would you expect but peace, when you're in the loving presence of God the gracious Father, God the loving Son, and God the interceding Holy Spirit?

Yours in his holy Name,

—⌐⌐

GOD'S GIFT OF TRUTH
FOR YOUR TIME WITH HIM

⨍ God honors your desire to come to him—
however you choose to come.

⨍ Faithfulness matters more to God than duration. But as you grow closer to the Lord,
chances are your time with him will grow.

⨍ If you let them, times of trouble can mature
your prayer life.

⨍ Prayer still works even when you're full of
questions. And don't be afraid to bring your
questions and doubts to the Lord.

⨍ Always remember to say thankyou when you
pray. It's not just a question of manners, but
of remembering how blessed you really are.

—⌐⌐

CHAPTER SIX

Cloudy,
with Patches of Sun

Let me hear joy and gladness; let the bones you have crushed rejoice. Hide your face from my sins and blot out all my iniquity. Create in me a pure heart, O God, and renew a steadfast spirit within me. Do not cast me from your presence or take your Holy Spirit from me. Restore to me the joy of your salvation and grant me a willing spirit, to sustain me.

—PSALM 51:8-12

For the LORD shall comfort Zion: he will comfort all her waste places; and he will make her wilderness like Eden, and her desert like the garden of the LORD; joy and glad-ness shall be found therein, thanksgiving, and the voice of melody....Therefore the redeemed of the LORD shall return, and come with singing unto Zion; and everlasting joy shall be upon their head: they shall obtain gladness and joy; and sorrow and mourning shall flee away.

—ISAIAH 51:3,11 KJV

I tell you the truth, you will weep and mourn while the world rejoices. You will grieve, but your grief will turn to joy. A woman giving birth to a child has pain because her time has come; but when her baby is born she forgets the anguish because of her joy that a child is born into the world. So with you: Now is your time of grief, but I will see you again and you will rejoice, and no one will take away your joy.

—JOHN 16:20-22

6

CLOUDY, WITH
PATCHES OF SUN

Finding comfort and joy in times of sorrow

＿ᑦ

I have to be honest with you. I didn't *like* having cancer.

The symptoms were frightening, annoying, and sometimes excruciating. The treatment was no fun at all. The side effects and related syndromes—such as the shingles—I could happily have lived without. I wasn't wild about the way the disease overturned and rearranged my life, and I really hated the long, dark, worrisome nights.

The truth is, there's just nothing inherently uplifting about a life-destroying disease or a painful course of treatment and, given the choice, I'd just as soon have avoided both. (I'm sure that someone suffering from clinical depression or a painful divorce or a devastating financial reversal would say something similar.)

So if you ask me whether my cancer journey was a joyful or a comforting experience, I'd have to say no.

But if you ask me whether I *experienced* comfort and joy during those four years, my answer would be different. For even in the midst of fear and pain and occasional despair, the comfort was real, the joy unmistakable, the hope unshaken.

Yes, there were periods of time when the blackness closed around me, when I saw no glimmers of joy in the dark, when the only comfort I could find was a feeble trust that life would not always be that way. There were moments when I literally didn't know how I would manage to endure. And during those times, I definitely wasn't feeling very cheerful!

But where does it say in Scripture that we are supposed to be always smiling, always cheerful, always "up"? If anything, the opposite is true. The Bible shoots absolutely straight about the bad things that happen in our lives—and it never pulls punches about how bad they can be. And it never asks the victims of evil to lie and put on a cheerful face.

Think of Job, stripped of his family, his possessions, and his health, sitting on a garbage heap and scraping his boils and refusing to agree with those who said he'd brought his problems on himself.

Think of David, hounded by his enemies, worried about his future, hiding in a cave and pouring his anguish out to the Lord in psalms.

Think of the Hebrews far from home, taken into exile, forced to sing cheerful songs in a foreign land when all they really wanted to do was wail.

Think of John the Baptist beheaded because of an old man's lust or Stephen stoned or Paul imprisoned for the crime of spreading the Good News.

Even more to the point, think of Jesus, hanging on a cross, with the weight of your sins and mine pulling down against flesh and bone and nerve endings as well as heart and soul.

Those are not cheerful events. They're not supposed to make us giggle. And neither are things like cancer and depression and disaster.

I keep thinking of that humorous cliché, "If you can stay calm, while all around you is chaos...then you probably haven't completely understood the situation." Well, there are times in life when, if you really feel chirpy or cheerful, you really haven't understood the situation. God doesn't like human suffering any more than he likes human sin. And being happy about the bad things in the world—even the bad things that cause us personal pain—is just plain inappropriate.

And yet...the Bible *does* tell us to be joyful, no matter what. It tells us that specifically and forcefully and repeatedly. As John Piper puts it in *Desiring God,* we are *commanded* to be joyful, so joylessness is really a form of disobedience. James 1:2 tells us that we should "Consider it pure joy...whenever [we] face trials of many kinds." The book of Philippians puts it even more directly: "Rejoice in the Lord always. I will say it again: Rejoice!" (Philippians 4:4).

The trick, of course, is *how* to do that. How do we manage to face our pain honestly and realistically and yet obey God's command to be joyful? When life is just awful, how do we live up to what Catholic activist Dorothy Day called "the duty of delight"?

Clearly, there's a difference between being joyfully obedient and being inappropriately cheerful in the face of real suffering and pain—and it's not just a matter of telling ourselves we ought to be happy when we're obviously not. The distinction is that we rejoice *in the midst* of our suffering, not *because* of it. And one of the reasons we rejoice is that we've been given a glimpse of the big picture. We know how it all comes out, so our overall attitude can be that of joy even when we're crying out in pain and fear and frustration.

Think about all the Bible stories I mentioned above. In almost all of them there is an undercurrent of joy to be found even amidst the pain. Not cheeriness. Not even happiness—again, the anguish is real. But still there is also a sense of deep, unmistakable comfort and rejoicing happening right alongside the anguish, and it's always because the good of what God is doing is so much better than any awful circumstance that can arise.

Job, even as he wallowed on his garbage heap, was still able to see his Lord face-to-face and to gasp in awe at the wonder of "things too wonderful for me to know" (Job 42:3).

David, though pursued by his enemies, became king of Israel and an ancestor of Jesus. He was a man who lived close to God. And though the sorrow in his psalms is heartfelt, the exuberant rejoicing in them outweighs the sadness.

The Hebrew people, even in exile, were not totally bereft of joy and comfort. They had memories and traditions to sustain them, the promises of the prophets to give them hope. John the Baptist had the joy of being the first to recognize the Messiah. Stephen was comforted with a joyful heavenly vision even as the stones flew. And Paul, in his imprisonment, was the one who told us he had learned to rejoice in *everything*.

Even Jesus, knowing his agonizing death was near, seemed to find a tender joy in celebrating Passover with his friends. And the horror of his crucifixion cannot be considered apart from the deep beauty of his loving sacrifice and the triumph of his resurrection. Good Friday sadness and Easter joy are two sides of one coin, and with God the toss will always (eventually) turn up heads.

In God's big picture, joy will prevail over sadness because God has won his cosmic battle over the forces of evil. Everything else that happens in this time in between that victory and God's final triumph is just a matter of cleaning up. That's the big picture that makes comfort and joy appropriate and desirable even in the face of great evil and suffering and pain.

Because of what God has done and is doing in the world and in my life, I really can take comfort. Because he will have the last word, it really is possible for me to rejoice—not because of my suffering, but in the midst of it. And because he is always present and working in my life, there are things I can celebrate even as I mourn. I can rejoice *in* my suffering because of what I know God is working through it to strengthen me and build my character. And I can rejoice *in spite of* my suffering because of what I know God is doing behind the scenes—which is bringing about my hopeful future.

That's the big picture. God is at work. God has won. All will be well. The trouble, of course, is that it's hard for us finite human beings to keep our eye on the big picture.

We've still got to live in our imperfect, mortal bodies amid a fallen humanity. We still have body cells that can run amuck, nerve endings that can fray, a variety of body systems that can break down. We still live in a world where innocents suffer, where men and women do unspeakable things to each other, where the earth shakes and the wind blows and sometimes we have to wait and wait and wait for things to get better. All of that means rejoicing will sometimes be a challenge. Comfort will sometimes be hard to find. And sometimes, when we're told to rejoice, we may feel like a child who has been told not only to eat her broccoli but to *like* it.

What needs to happen, in other words, is for us not only to *understand* all will be well, but to convince our hearts and our souls and our spirits of that joyful reality. And that really can happen. Feeling happy may not always be appropriate, but it really is possible to find comfort and consolation and, yes, real feelings of joy in the midst of our painful times.

Even when I most hated having cancer, I found that to be true. That simple fact was crucial because it helped me keep a positive attitude—and it's widely known that positive thinking is a source of strength and healing. Comfort and joy are not just nice extras for our lives. We need them. They give us strength. They heal us and make us free. If—once again—we can find them amid our pain.

"The joy of the LORD is your strength," said Nehemiah when he was attempting to reestablish Jewish worship and culture in Judea near the end of the Hebrews' time of exile (see Nehemiah 8:10). He was reminding his people that celebrating God's goodness actually opens the way for God to work more freely. And this verse came to me again and again when I felt the weakest—possibly because it supported all the medical research that shows a hopeful, joyful, upbeat person has a better chance of winning against cancer than a worried, sad, morose one. (I even discovered that the original meaning of the English word *comfort* also has to do with strength—it comes from the same word as *fortress*.)

So how did I manage to find that strengthening, healing comfort and joy in my life even during the dark, painful experiences of diagnosis and treatment?

First, I really did try to keep my focus on the big picture, to hang on to a sense of what God was doing in my life and how he was working for good. Bob and I tried to do this together. And it wasn't always easy; we found there's nothing like a personal crisis to narrow your vision. But it helped to steep ourselves in Scripture, to remind ourselves again and again of the ways God has worked in the past and of his promises for the future. It helped to talk to each other and to other Christians, not with nagging "cheer up" messages but with reminders of what God has done and is doing. Prayer helped a lot, too, opening our hearts to the direct presence and work of the Lord. (Remember, the Holy Spirit is known as the Comforter, and joy is a specific fruit of the Spirit!)

It also helped, I found, to redefine rejoicing in my own mind. I think most of us are so conditioned to thinking of joy as just a positive feeling that we have a hard time finding it when our feelings are negative. But I found that when I changed my feelings about joy it began to feel more possible.

To me, joy is a sense of being glad and grateful that the universe—and my whole life—is under God's care and that ultimately everything is going to be all right. It's a feeling, but it's also a *knowing*—like going through a horrible day with the secret knowledge that something good is going on behind the scenes. And it's an attitude we can choose, like gratitude. Or gladness.

I found that focusing on gladness, in fact, can be a helpful key to finding joy. In the Bible, *joy* and *gladness* are often mentioned together, almost in the same breath, as part of the same reality. (A quick search with a concordance will show just how often the two words are paired.) And I found that during those times when I couldn't come up with any feelings of joy, I could almost always manage gladness about good things I knew to be true.

I am glad I have a husband, for example—and a good, loving one at that. And that's true whether I'm feeling joyful about my marriage or not.

I am glad I have a family who is finally at peace with one another. Also true, no matter what.

I am truly glad my cancer is happening now, when they've made such progress, and not ten years ago, when my particular diagnosis would have been an automatic death sentence.

On a more cosmic scale, I am glad God sent Jesus to earth, that he loves me, that he wants to heal me. I am glad I have the promise of everlasting life.

Maybe it's a word game, but keeping this distinction between joy and gladness helps me balance honesty with obedience. When rejoicing feels forced and happiness seems out of the question, I can still be honestly glad. And if gladness is part of rejoicing—then I really can rejoice no matter what.

The idea of gladness also helps me because it helps me keep looking, once again, at the big picture. Even when I was on my knees in the bathroom, or watching my hair fall out in clumps, or trying to find relief from the agony of shingles by lying absolutely still and barely breathing, I could still be honestly glad that God was in my life. I could still muster heartfelt thankfulness (and gladness is closely related to gratitude) when I thought of scriptural promises of hope, when I remembered how many people were praying for me, when I took to heart the big-picture reality that good things were still happening, the prayers that were being answered.

Another part of the big picture that helped me keep on rejoicing in the midst of my pain was a sense that there was purpose in my pain. I found that a positive attitude about my treatment was far easier to maintain when I reminded myself that the same procedures that were nauseating me or causing my cheeks to swell were also helping me heal. And a positive attitude about the cancer itself was easier to come by when I reminded myself that God not only was working out his purposes *in spite of* my current circumstances, but that he was actually *using* those circumstances to make me better—stronger, kinder, bolder, more patient, more prayerful.

Scriptures assured me this was true, and on my better days I could actually see it happening. I could see the changes in my character, and I was beginning to get a vision for a whole new kind of ministry to hurting women. When I kept my eye on God's big picture, the meaning and purpose I found there was enough to bring me comfort and make me glad—just as the promise of a baby is enough to keep a woman thinking joyfully (more or less) through the pain of childbirth.

But focusing on meaning and purpose and the big picture was not the only thing that helped me rejoice and find comfort in the midst of the dark times in my life. Interestingly enough, I was also helped by celebrating the *small picture*—the little moments of true happiness that persisted throughout the dark days of my illness.

Even on the darkest days, you see, I often experienced patches of sun. There was beauty. There were jokes. There were sweet times of fellowship, hopeful gladness, reprieves from pain. It was not a happy time, but I did sometimes feel happy. I did experience feelings of comfort and joy. And for me, such little moments of joy were often more powerful than the larger truths in keeping my spirit upbeat.

I don't know why this was true. Perhaps it was because my mind and body were often not up to the task of grasping weighty truths and could only latch on to little ones. Perhaps it was simply because I was less busy and paying better attention. But I do know that even though I rejoiced in the big picture of my salvation and the redemption of the world, even though I depended utterly on the reality that God was sovereign and was at work bringing good out of my circumstances—it was the tiny pleasures that often lifted me out of my pain and despair.

The lilting sound of flute music played next door. (At first I thought it was a radio, but it turned out to be my neighbor at the Residence Inn.)

A hug from my smallest grandson—or my nearly grown-up granddaughter—that felt like an infusion of youth and strength.

A honeysuckle vine blooming outside my window or the sound of waves crashing on the beach.

A cartoon on the clinic bulletin board—or a vampire joke from the good-natured nurse who drew my blood.

A letter from a reader who has named her baby Emilie—spelling it just the way I do. (As of this writing, I have at least ten little namesakes—including my good friend Yoli's beautiful grandbaby!)

Bob's beloved voice reading Scriptures of joy and praise and promise out loud to me.

Why are such little joys so powerful? I think it's because they remind us that the whole fabric of life, which includes suffering, is not only woven by God but full of his presence. His kingdom is in the present as well as in the future. God is doing his work here, now—in the natural world, in our relationships, in *us*. Life doesn't stop, goodness and beauty don't go away. We are here on this earth to *live*—and that remains true no matter what else is happening in our lives. Not even sickness and pain and tragedy can blot out the true joy that shines in the tapestry of our lives. Even the darkest clouds can't keep those patches of sun from shining through.

Ironically, I've found, it sometimes takes sickness and pain and tragedy to give us eyes to see this joy and comfort that's built into our most mundane moments. Taking joy in the days God sends us is part of our daily call to obedience. We are called to notice the beauty around us, to really see God's hand at work. And while pain and suffering can make that difficult, the enforced stillness that comes with many difficult periods of life can also make noticing and appreciating easier.

In my experience, at least, I found it helped to try. When I could manage to look out the window and enjoy the view or sit with my eyes closed and listen to something beautiful or let my memory of a scriptural truth fill my heart, I did experience joy. Not usually delirious, buoyant happiness, but a quiet recognition that no matter what was happening in the cells of my body, the world was still beautiful, and God was still at work in it.

Sometimes finding the joy required keeping an open mind—because pain or illness or depression can change the way we experience the world. When I was on chemo, for instance, I lost much of my sense of taste, so it was difficult for me to enjoy delicious food. However, the knowledge that Bob and my children and grandchildren and friends were trying hard to find something to please my palate and build my strength brought me the deeper joy of knowing how deeply I was loved.

As I look back on my cancer years, in fact, I realize that they included major joys as well as little pleasures. Hearing my daughter pray for me for the first time in her life was an unforgettable joy. Seeing my Bob come through like the hero he is—and realizing just how deeply I can trust his love—was a constant source of joy. Knowing for certain that our witness in our time of pain resulted in at least one soul's coming to the Lord—that's enough to make me jump up and down and shout. And finally being pronounced cancer free—that was a joy that resonated through my whole life.

My point is that the joy is there—whether we feel it or remember it. It's planted deep in our lives, and it will grow and flourish if we give it the slightest attention. It's in the big picture of what God is doing in the universe, and it's in the small picture of our moments and our days. The trick is not just to feel it—but to open our hearts to it.

In Thornton Wilder's play *Our Town* a young girl who has died (her name is Emily!) looks back on her life and asks, "Does any human being ever realize life while they live it, every minute?" I think that I'm just now learning the nuances of that joyful lesson—and my illness and pain have been my teachers.

Because my medication made so much of my food taste awful, I treasure the ability to once more enjoy colorful vegetables and luscious cookies.

Because I spent so many hours confined to quarters—I treasure every breath of fresh air, every glimpse of the ocean or mountains...and every trip to Target!

Because I almost lost them, I treasure every moment with my family, grandchildren, friends, and neighbors.

I look at so many things differently now—look at every experience as a gift from God, a lesson, an enrichment in my life. I think "I may never see that again." And this is not just a recent development. Even in the very midst of my cancer treatment, I was discovering the preciousness—yes, even the joy—of life. I remember feeling almost guilty when I'd fall asleep during a visit from my grandkids. I didn't want to miss any of it.

I don't want you to miss it, either. I want you to know that in times of illness, times of pain, through cloudy days and dark midnights, the joy is there—no matter what.

Comfort is there, no matter what. If that's hard for us to feel sometimes, it's because of our limitations, not God's lack of provision. In fact, it's in our very limitations that God does his greatest work.

I discovered that back in the days when I was hanging on for dear life to the joyful truth of God's promises. Psalm 30:5 tells us "weeping may remain for a night, but rejoicing comes in the morning." And sometimes, in those days of midnight darkness, all I could honestly do was cling to the Lord and wait for dawn, wait for him to bring me a joy I just couldn't manage on my own.

But those were the days when I was reminded that joy was never intended to be something I achieved. It's a gift of the Lord, a fruit of the Spirit, a flash of brightness in my cloudy todays and a brilliant promise of tomorrow.

Joyfulness might be a command, in other words, but God never commands what he doesn't enable. God will bring us the reminders we need about the big picture. He will give us the small-picture flashes of happiness even in hard times. He will open our eyes to see the beauty that permeates all of our life, the heart to be glad and grateful. He will grow us into joy after joy—until the day when sorrow and mourning really are no more.

So we don't really have to worry about rejoicing. All we have to do is trust the Lord, to remember all he has done, all that he is doing, all that he is.

But then, the only response that makes any sense will be what he wanted for us all the time: joy!

MY DEAR FRIEND IN CHRIST,

If you are going through a dark and joyless period of your life, I want to give you a message. It's a message that weaves itself all through God's Word, and it holds the secret of the joy you need.

It's a message of promise—that things will get better, that you have a future, that your life has a purpose.

It's a message of companionship—that you're loved, that you're not the only one going through this, that others have felt this way, too, and lived through it, and emerged stronger and more joyful.

Most of all, it's a message of truth, of what's real and lasting. The truth is that God is in charge. He's in the very fabric of your days, in every cell of your body as well as in every star in the universe. God knows what he's doing. He will see you through. He will strengthen you and bring you joy.

I hope you can hear this message today, take it deeply to heart, and make it part of your life. But if you forget, you can hear it again—in holy Scripture, in the love of other people, in the words of wise counselors, in the whispers of the Holy Spirit.

Open your ears.

Open your eyes.

Most of all open your heart—to the beautiful joy the Lord is waiting to give you.

Joyfully yours—really!

Emilie

GOD'S GIFT OF TRUTH WHEN YOU NEED SOME COMFORT AND JOY

♭ It's impossible to be always happy, but it really is possible to be continually joyful.

♭ Little joys can carry you through when you can't get your mind or body around big ones.

♭ You can *be* joyful even when you don't *feel* joyful. You can *accept* comfort even when you don't *feel* comfortable.

♭ When you don't feel comfort, look for strength. When you don't feel strong, give the Lord your weakness.

♭ Joy comes from understanding what has been promised, trusting in God's care, practicing thanksgiving—and appreciating life.

♭ God will give you the comfort and joy you need, in the proper dosages, to bring you where you need to be.

♭ Joy is that deep-down knowledge that all is well, regardless, and all shall be well, no matter what.

CHAPTER SEVEN

Hand In Heart In Hand

Then the righteous will answer him, "Lord, when did we see you hungry and feed you, or thirsty and give you something to drink? When did we see you a stranger and invite you in, or needing clothes and clothe you? When did we see you sick or in prison and go to visit you?" The King will reply, "I tell you the truth, whatever you did for one of the least of these brothers of mine, you did for me."

—MATTHEW 25:37-40

A new command I give you: Love one another. As I have loved you, so you must love one another. By this all men will know that you are my disciples, if you love one another.

—JOHN 13:34-35

Praise be to God and Father of our Lord Jesus Christ, the Father of compassion and the God of all comfort, who comforts us in all our troubles, so that we can comfort those in any trouble with the comfort we ourselves have received from God. For just as the sufferings of Christ flow over into our lives, so also through Christ our comfort overflows.

—2 CORINTHIANS 1:3-5

7

HAND IN HEART IN HAND

The healing ministry of loving relationships

—◌—

Did you know that Jesus lives in cancer clinics?

I know it's true, because I've seen him there. I've heard his voice. I've felt his tender touch, even in the most frightening moments of my treatment.

Our Lord Christ walks the sterile corridors with a bald head and puffy face, with scars from surgery and IV drips hanging from his arms. Sometimes he wears a hospital badge and a clinician's coat. Sometimes he sits in waiting rooms or keeps watch at bedsides.

His hands are the hands that scrub bathrooms or make soup or copy Scripture into a notecard. His feet are the feet that make rounds or mow the grass for someone else. His eyes are the eyes that notice needs and attend to them. He speaks love over long-distance lines; his heart shines from handwritten cards and hastily typed e-mails.

And sometimes—miracle of miracles—the Lord's voice is my own feeble, croaky one speaking words of compassion and encouragement to someone else who is traveling in this "world of woe."

From our sojourn in Cancerland, Bob and I have learned anew the truth that Teresa of Avila wrote more than four hundred years ago:

> *Christ has no body now on earth but yours; yours are the only hands through which he can do his work, yours are the only feet with which he can go about the world, yours are the only eyes through which his compassion can shine forth upon a troubled world. Christ has no body now on earth but yours.*

For it was so often through the hands and the feet and the eyes and the hearts of so many of God's people—the literal body of Christ—that we received the blessings of God's care during my illness. And at the same time, we found that we were called to embody Christ's love to others even in our time of need, to use our own hands and feet and eyes and hearts in the Lord's service.

In the midst of the darkest journey of our life, in other words, we found not only comfort and help, but a whole new ministry.

I don't know why that surprised me, but it did. When we canceled the last of my seminars and focused our energies on healing, I guess I thought we would take a break from ministry. But apparently that's not the way the Lord works. Instead, he kept on putting people in our path— people who needed love, needed help, needed prayer. And as we acted in concern for others and in obedience to the

Lord's promptings, we saw God work through us, even as we felt his love embodied in the care and concern of so many who loved and cared for us.

So we were relearning a truth we had always known, which is that God usually chooses the imperfect but lovely vehicle of humanity to accomplish his loving work in the world. On the surface, it seems like such an inefficient way to get things done. After all, human beings are fickle, selfish, and sinful. We let each other down at least as much as we lift each other up.

And it's not as if God couldn't do his work without our help. He can do anything—and at times, I believe, he does intervene supernaturally and directly in our lives.

And yet what better way to reach and to teach his wayward children than to use our hands and our hearts to show his love to one another? Surely that's one reason God became a human in the first place—to teach us with human hands, in a way we could truly understand. He's still doing his work on earth in human form, only now he does it through our hearts, our hands.

Years ago, a dear friend of Jenny's, a lovely girl named Lynn, was diagnosed with cancer and about to undergo a bone marrow transplant—an even more dangerous and experimental procedure back then than it is now. To encourage her and show support, I hosted a little luncheon for Lynn and some friends. After enjoying our meal and dessert, we all gathered round the table for a little project.

We had Lynn trace her hand on five sheets of paper, one for each guest. We then drew heart shapes on "our" handprints and decorated the pages with markers. We all placed our hands on Lynn's and prayed together for her healing. Then we each took our individual handprint home and posted it on the refrigerator door. Whenever we passed through our kitchens we would be reminded to place our hands on "hers" and lift our hearts in prayer to the Father on her behalf. (Today Lynn has been cancer free for ten years.)

Ever since then, that image of a heart on a hand has been especially meaningful to me because it reminds me of the kind of person-to-person ministry we're all called to carry out. I have used it in my prayer notebook, asking people I want to pray for to trace their hands on a page in my book. (Now my prayer notebook waves with hands and hearts from fellow cancer fighters.) I have taught it to children and shared it in my seminars. When the news began to spread of my cancer and so many people called and wrote and offered to pray, the little heart-in-hand symbol seemed a perfect way to communicate. So I traced my own hand on a piece of paper. I drew a little heart on the handprint, added a hopeful Scripture, a brief summary of what was going on with me, and a simple request for prayer. Below that, Bob added a more detailed update about my condition. Then we made copies of that simple sheet of paper and sent it out to all the people who had offered to pray for us. We even posted copies on our website (www.emiliebarnes.com) to function as a kind of newsletter. "Hold my hand," those little messages read, "as you pray for my healing."

Heart to heart, hand to hand—I believe that's how God intends for us to relate to each other. I believe that whatever the Lord calls us to, he will make possible. And that's why I believe that if we give our lives to Jesus, three things are going to happen:

First, there will be someone who extends Christ's love *to* us.

Second, there will be someone who needs to know Christ's love *through* us.

And third, there'll always be someone watching and learning about the way Christ's love can change the world.

That may sound unrealistic or simplistic, but I think it's true.

I really believe, for instance, that if we place our trust in the Lord, he will see that we get what we need in terms of love, support, encouragement, and help. I don't mean we'll always have all the friends we want and need at any given time. There may be times when we feel lonely or isolated, or when our chief sources of love and support come from a distance, or from memories, or even from books. Sometimes the people who love us are not the sort of people we would pick as friends, and sometimes they don't act the way you want them to. (Have you ever been in a church where you actively liked and enjoyed everybody there?) But still, if we trust the Lord, I believe we have sufficient human love in our life to equip us for his kingdom.

And this, of course, brings us to the second thing we can expect from the Lord if we give our life to him: our ministry to others. No matter where we are, there will always be something specific we can do to embody Christ's love to another human being. No matter where we go, there'll always be somebody to care about.

It may be an elderly person down the street who needs help with home repairs. It might be a harried coffee shop waitress who could use a kind word. It may be a young person who needs to hear about the Lord or a child who needs a ball game or a story. Wherever we go, we'll meet people who are lonely, people who are needy, people who need to experience God's love and his salvation. There will always be opportunities to "do unto the least" of our fellow human beings—to touch them with the Lord's hands, speak to them with the Lord's voice, listen to them with the Lord's ears.

This kind of ministry comes in addition to any other call the Lord may have on our lives. And it's not optional. Saying yes to this kind of loving, specific ministry is as vital to our spiritual and emotional well-being as receiving the care of those who love us. It's part of the image of God in us, and we ignore it to our peril.

If we follow Christ, then, we also follow his call to be his hands and feet and heart to those around us. And that's when the third truth comes into play—that someone will be watching. We may be acutely aware of being observed, or we may never notice, but someone will be affected by our example. By this means the Lord takes our simple loaves and fishes of caring and kindness and multiplies them in the world—yet another kind of miracle that's easy to miss in the course of our daily lives.

If we have children, for example, they will watch what we do for others and learn what God's love is all about. If we have unbelieving friends, they may draw conclusions about our God by the way we act toward other people. With every human transaction we make, we are preaching a sermon about God's love.

This is important stuff—loving and caring for people, being supporting and encouraging, modeling the love of Christ for the world. It's the heart of ministry. And ministry is for all Christians—ordained or laity, old or young, healthy and vigorous or struggling with illness—even Christians in cancer clinics. All of which raises the question of *how* we minister to each other and show love to others in the name of Christ.

After my time in Cancerland, I'm more acutely aware than ever of the many different ways we can do this. After all, I've been on the receiving end of such extravagant giving—I know firsthand how it can work. I've also watched my Bob minister in love to those all around us, and I've done my best to answer God's call as well. And from this experience I've observed some of the more helpful ways we human beings can minister to one another even in times of crisis and difficulty—or *especially* in times of crisis or difficulty.

One of the most basic and helpful forms of ministry, I've found, is one that sometimes isn't even recognized as a ministry. It's a way of showing love by simply *seeing* others—recognizing their importance, paying attention, listening to them.

My Bob had a wonderful "seeing" ministry while we were living in the Seattle Residence Inn, and I believe it made an impact for the kingdom, even if part of it did come from social starvation. I know Bob was often lonely and bored while we were going through that segment of my treatment; I was often heavily medicated and slept through large portions of every day, leaving Bob to fend for himself. I woke up from a nap one day and heard him talking to someone in the other room who ended up being the window washer. Bob managed to turn his loneliness into a ministry by reaching out to every one around us—not only our fellow patients, but also the hotel bell staff, the desk clerks, the food-service personnel, the shuttle bus drivers, and the clinic staff.

Bob would learn their names, ask them about their lives, remember what they told him. To the best of my physical ability, I tried to do the same. But it wasn't until we went back to Seattle for my one-year checkup that we realized what a powerful impression this simple ministry of seeing had made. Everywhere we went we encountered smiles, and even the kitchen staff came out to greet us. In a world where so many people feel anonymous and unappreciated, the simple act of noticing other people and treating them like someone had made a significant impact.

But of course there's more to ministry than simply noticing people. Often, I believe, we're called to a ministry of *practical caring*—doing what we can to meet the needs of others. Many of my doctors and nurses, of course, were fully involved in this ministry. And we patients also did what we could to take care of each other. We passed around vital information: what foods go down best after chemo, how to find the best value in wigs, how to bathe when you're too weak to get out of the tub. We shared war stories, inspiring poems, healthy recipes. Those who were at the market or the pharmacy picked up groceries or non-prescription medicines for those who couldn't get there. Those who were relatively healthy did what we could to help those who were weak.

If all that sounds clichéd, let me hasten to add that such mutual caring is no more automatic in cancer circles than it is in the larger world. Not everybody in those clinics reached out to others. I met plenty who were cynical or bitter or selfish in their anger. But these were the ones who suffered the most—because they put themselves outside the circle of hands and hearts that brought hope to so many of us.

My family and friends, of course, were fully involved in the ministry of caring. Every day of my cancer journey, I felt the Lord's love flowing through those he called to care for me. Bob's care, for instance, was truly a matter of saying yes to ministry and not just doing what came naturally. He was raised in a traditional home with very traditional gender roles. Though we have always worked as equal partners in our home, his domain has always been business and yard work while keeping the house and cooking the meals were always my primary responsibilities. When I became sick, I honestly had no idea who would care for us in these areas.

But for four long years, my very traditional husband not only kept our books and watered the lawn, he also shopped for groceries, prepared three meals a day, kept the house straight, and cleaned up after me. He kept track of my medications, held my hand in endless waiting rooms, and held my head in a succession of rest rooms. I say without reservation that during the darkest days of my illness, my Bob was not only a faithful husband, but the hands and heart of Christ.

But perhaps because I was aware of how much stress Bob's new job put on him, I was also doubly aware of the friends and family members who took on themselves the ministry of caring for *both* of us. Some brought food or arrived at the house just in time to save Bob from cooking a meal. Others showed up to helped Bob with the housework or to sit with me while he took a well-deserved break. Our children and grandchildren showed up on a regular basis to clean or run errands or to take care of big projects like painting our new house so we could move in.

Often, one of these special people chose a specific ministry of caring to carry out over a period of time. My friend Yoli, for example, came over to cut my hair when going out might endanger my weakened immune system. And Anissa Otto, the daughter of our friends Donna and David, who lives in Seattle, volunteered for the specific ministry of doing our laundry while we were in Seattle. Every Tuesday she picked up our dirty clothes, washed and ironed them, and delivered them back to the hotel. What a love gift that was to us.

And so many others just came to visit, to spend time with us and share our load by simply being there. We found them as important as haircuts and the laundry, especially during those times when I was unable to be good company for Bob.

One of the blessings that came with our move to Newport Beach was that Bob found a group of truly supportive Christian male friends there. These were mostly old friends, and they provided a kind of prayerful support group that our travel schedule had made difficult to find in Riverside. A simple visit from one of this group—a little "guy talk," perhaps a football game on TV—did wonders for Bob's spirits.

In addition, we used to laugh about Bob's "dates," which afforded him a lot of enjoyment during the times when I was more or less out of commission. Bob enjoys female company—it's one of the reason the women who attend my seminars relate to him so well. Bob is also a very social person who loves to talk, loves to go out. So during our time in Seattle, especially, a procession of women friends would arrive to visit and end up going out with Bob for dinner or shopping. Their company for my steadfast but weary husband was truly a ministry of caring for me— and besides, they often brought home something yummy, like beautiful vegetables, from the Pike Place Market!

In visits like these, of course, our friends were offering us more than practical care. They were also offering *encouragement*, which is a powerful and necessary kind of ministry. Three times at least in the New Testament (1 Thessalonians 5:11; Hebrews 3:13; 10:25) Christians are told specifically to encourage one another, and many other verses give the same message through different words. Because of our human limitations, because sin is real, because life can be so hard, we are all subject to discouragement. We all have times when we need the message of "All will be well," of "You can do it," of "Get up and try again"—especially when the clouds seem heavy and we're traveling an uphill road.

I cannot begin to tell of the value and beauty of the encouraging cards and faxes and phone calls we received from all over the country—from that first big box of cards from Bailey Smith Ministries to the elaborate posters crafted by my grandchildren to the cheerful messages left by friends every day on my answering machine. People I barely knew—or had never even met—lifted my spirits by telling stories of hope, sharing Scriptures, and promising to pray for me.

One thing I have learned about this ministry from all these loving people is that encouragement can take many forms. A cheerful note is great, but it's not the only—or even the most effective—way to help somebody up or move them along.

My friend Barbara DeLorenzo, for instance, encourages me by her sweetness and her faithfulness and her willingness to do whatever she can to make me feel better. She is always ready with a hug, and she gives the best foot rubs in the state.

My son, Brad, encourages me with little loving challenges. One Christmas when I was really sick and discouraged, he chided me that I hadn't made him his snowball cookies that year—the cookies I had made him every Christmas since he was tiny. Well, I knew Brad wasn't really worried about the cookies. (If you could see his trim, taut waistline, you'd know cookies aren't a big part of his life.) But Brad understands me very well, and he knew that asking for those cookies was a way of telling me not to give up. Well, I knew perfectly well what he was doing—but it worked. I got off the couch, made those cookies, and started fighting a little harder for my life. He got his cookies the next year, too, and he'll get them every year I can possibly make them!

And my friend Donna Otto encourages me partly by her honesty. Because I trust her to tell me the truth, her words of hope reach me with extra power.

I remember a time when I was distraught over having to go through another chemo session. "I don't know if I can make it another time," I told Donna tearfully. And instead of giving me "You'll be fine" platitudes, she put her arms around me and said, "If God chooses to give you fewer days than what we'd like, I will see to it personally that you will be comfortable." I found her directness a form of encouragement because it cut to the heart of my fears. Realizing my friend was willing to care for me no matter what helped give me the strength I needed to move forward with the treatment.

Honesty, then, can be a form of encouragement when it is steeped in love. So can humor and fun, which can bring me hope even when I don't really feel like laughing. My dear old friends Yoli Brogger and Florence Littauer are especially good at getting a smile out of me and lifting my spirits; so are Jenny and my exuberantly sanguine grandson Chad. And I learned during my many hours in waiting rooms and clinic offices that laughter is a true lifeline in any situation where pain is a fixture and death seems to loom. While jokes about catheters and skewed wigs might seem a bit tasteless, those of us who were coping with the discomforts of cancer treatment found them both empowering and encouraging—almost a way of thumbing our nose at the powers of darkness. Anyone who could make me laugh was a powerful encourager to me, even when my shingles made laughing a literal pain!

A ministry of encouragement, in fact, comes in as many forms as there are people. But surely a special kind of encouragement comes from those who can say, "I've been there. I understand what you're going through. Everything will be all right."

It's been interesting to me recently to realize that my dearest friends in the world all came from very dysfunctional families—all were deeply wounded as young women. I didn't consciously set out to find them, but our spirits seemed to call to one another. Because my father was an alcoholic who flew into drunken rages, because my uncle abused me, because my aunt manipulated and browbeat me, I know what it is like to be betrayed by those I loved, and I feel a special solidarity to women in similar situations. And because I have experienced a measure of healing for this past pain, I find I can be an effective encourager for those who struggle with similar kinds of pain. I can testify to the reality of God's healing for broken relationships and old resentments. I can witness that it *is* possible and spiritually necessary to move toward forgiveness and reconciliation.

In much the same way, during my cancer years I especially appreciated the encouragement of cancer survivors who understood what I was going through and cared enough to share a word of hope. Even those who were just a little ahead of me in the treatment cycle could help by saying, "The hair does grow back" or "The shingles do diminish as your immune system grows stronger" or just "I feel that way, too." Such encouraging words helped me so much I determined to pass them along to those who are going through what I've already finished. I've even come to believe that survivors of any significant trauma have a special call to encourage those who come behind us. Our very battle scars give us special credentials for honest and practical encouragement.

Many of the friends who encouraged me, of course, also prayed for me, and prayer in itself is an important form of ministry—a ministry I could manage even when I was too weak to help in any other way. And this very reality of weakness points to a surprising but very important form of ministry—a ministry of need.

Every human being, I believe, has a built-in desire to give, to help, to show love. It's part of the image of God within us, and it persists even through sin and selfishness. Helping others simply feels good, and many of us "strong" types find helping more pleasant than being helped. To be the needy one is hard because it humbles us; it grates against our illusions of self-sufficiency.

And yet one of the things I learned when I was sick was that I could bless others by allowing them to help me and even by asking for their help—and also, of course, by showing my gratitude for what they did. I didn't have to be effusive in my thanks or make immediate plans to pay them back in kind. In fact, it was better if I didn't put too much emphasis on reciprocating their kindness. I just had to receive graciously and gratefully and let them enjoy the satisfaction of helping.

I didn't become the kind of invalid who rings a little bell and requires everyone else to wait on her. Even in my weakest times, I wanted to do what I could to help myself. But when I shared my tears with my friends, when I let them crawl up on the bed with me and comfort me, we both were comforted. When I asked my grandchildren for help in getting a necessary chore done and showed my gratitude when they did it, we both felt good about the result. When I was honest about what I couldn't do and asked for help, I received the gift of love and care and my helper knew the joy of being an instrument of God's grace.

Quite a few years ago, I read a very moving magazine article about a young woman with the courage to give her friends that blessing. Her name was Susan Farrow. Stricken with a dangerous form of cancer and without family nearby, she asked several of her friends to walk with her on the cancer journey. This group of working women—who were practically strangers at the time—made a pact to be Susan's joint caregivers. For nearly four years they took turns cleaning, preparing meals, helping with doctor's appointments, and staying with Susan when she couldn't stay alone. In the process, they forged a unique sisterhood. And even though Susan finally succumbed to the disease, her willingness to acknowledge her need brought all of these friends a special blessing. "I learned what it was to put yourself in someone else's place," one of them said later. "I learned that by accepting limitations, you make life a richer experience. And I learned that people can be healed even if they are not cured."[3]

Isn't that a wonderful quality of our Lord—that his blessings flow most abundantly when we open our hands widely to receive? I even wonder if this was one of the secrets to Jesus' Sermon on the Mount, when he talked about happiness coming to the poor in spirit, the grieving, the meek, and so on. Such humble souls have the advantage of not being determined to do everything themselves, so they allow others to help them—and everyone is blessed!

Acknowledging our need and receiving help graciously, I believe, is a valid and wonderful kind of ministry. But that is not to downplay the beauty of giving—especially sacrificial giving. There are times in everyone's life, I believe, when we are called to give up a measure of our own comfort out of compassion for others and obedience to God. Such a ministry of *sacrifice*—giving until it hurts—can be difficult, but it can also transform lives in a way that ordinary giving can't approach.

When I think of such sacrifice, I think of my Bob first, of course. He has truly fulfilled his vow to be with me for better or worse, richer or poorer, in sickness and in health, till death do us part. I also think of Jenny, who volunteered a year out of her busy life to helping us—coming over daily to do what she could. I think of our friends Donna and David Otto, who flew in regularly from Phoenix at their own expense just to be with Bob and me and help us. I even think of myself—of the times when I felt sick but still forced myself to go out with my bored, lonely husband. And I can't help but think of Dan Rapoi, the young Canadian who chose to donate his bone marrow to save the life of a perfect stranger.

My first question after I met Dan, in fact, was "Why did you do that?" It turned out that in the city where he lived there was someone who needed a transplant, so they asked people to sign up and be tested. Dan, who works as a disk jockey, helped get the word out, so it just seemed natural for him to go in and be tested, too. Though he wasn't a match for that particular person, the data bank saved his name and his results—and our data bank search brought him up as a match for me. By that time I was extremely ill and waiting for a yes or no that could mean life or death for me. When they called, Dan's answer was yes. "How can I refuse such a great opportunity to help someone else?" he said.

Though donating bone marrow is not quite as invasive a procedure as donating, say, a kidney or a lung, it's still a lot more complicated than giving blood. It's a surgical procedure in which bone marrow is removed from the back of the pelvic bone through a series of small incisions. Donors incur risks from anesthesia and infection. And there is some pain as well. Dan told me he was sore and tired and was off work for about a week. The fact that this Christian young man was willing to go through all that just for the possibility of helping a complete stranger awes me. His was a true ministry of sacrifice.

Dan, of course, says that the sacrifice wasn't that big, and that the discomfort was balanced by the blessings that come from helping someone. And I really do understand a little of what he means—although I'm still amazed that he would do what he did for a woman he didn't even know. His reward in heaven for such sacrificial service will be great.

In the meantime, though, our family was determined to increase his blessing by showing our gratitude. Even before we were allowed to know Dan's name, we all sat down and wrote him a letter, telling him about us and thanking him for what he had done and trying to give him an idea of just how much love he had unleashed in the world through that one act of sacrificial service. As soon as we knew who he was, we sent our letters together in a fat envelope.

I have copies of all those letters now in my files—from little Weston's crayoned pictures through almost-grown granddaughter Christine's amazingly mature note, from Jenny's beautifully exuberant thank-you to Brad's thoughtful letter. Jenny made writing the notes a family project. And Brad, who tends to be a very private person, even gave me permission to read what he wrote. The process of expressing our thank-yous was fun and fulfilling for all of us—and I hope that Dan was blessed as well through what we shared. Whether our letters made a difference or not, surely the act of sacrificial giving brought him the deep satisfaction of living out Christ's redeeming purposes in the world.

And this brings me to the final kind of ministry all Christians are called to, in whatever circumstances we find ourselves—which is to bear witness to the life-changing power of Jesus Christ. Whenever we notice people, help them, encourage them, pray for them, or give of ourselves to make life better for them—and do it openly in the name of Christ—we participate in bringing God's kingdom to fulfillment.

The longer I live, the more pain and evil I've seen in this world, the more I've come to believe that simply being a witness to God's love and redemption is the most important ministry any of us will ever be called to do. And we're all called to do it—every day of our lives.

I'm not talking about preaching at people or arguing with them or haranguing them. But I'm not talking about just being nice to them, either. I believe we are called to love with the Lord's heart, helping with the Lord's hands, and then sharing boldly with those we meet about the Lord's gift of salvation.

All of us, every day of our lives, are presented with opportunities to do just that with the people around us— and our seasons of strength and plenty are a good time to develop the habit. But in Cancerland, I found, the opportunities arrive with even greater poignancy, because they often are matters of life and death. Though cancer is an awful disease in many ways, it does offer the advantage of stripping away pretenses and bringing important issues to the forefront. Witnessing was often easier around a treatment center, I found, because people who are facing death are more open to discussing life-or-death issues.

My only true regrets from my cancer years, in fact, involve times when I wasn't bold enough in sharing Christ with people who really needed him. I remember one woman in particular who sat next to me on the shuttle bus to the Hutch. Her eyes were full of such fear and such pain and such anger I couldn't help praying for her. We talked a little, and I discovered she was Jewish. She claimed to believe in God, but there was no peace about her. We chatted a bit longer, but I was feeling especially tired that day, so I let our conversation lag. I found out later that she had passed away, and I was haunted by the agitation I had sensed in her spirit. I thought, "Why wasn't I bolder with her? Why didn't I tell her about Jesus?"

Some of my sweetest memories, on the other hand, come from times when I did offer a direct witness. I remember one couple in particular. Jim and Barb, a couple from Iowa, had come to Seattle for Barb's bone marrow transplant, and she wasn't doing well. As we got to know them better and spent some time together, we started talking to them casually about God. Then one night we ran into them at dinner and invited them up to our suite for dessert. When we were finished, Bob said simply, "Let's just pray together." Then we joined hands and prayed—quietly and sweetly. Bob and I didn't think much of that time; it was pretty normal for us. But we got a note from her the next day to say that no one had ever prayed with them, nor had they ever prayed together.

We gave Jim and Barb one of our books, and we have kept in touch by mail, apprising each other of our progress in healing. Barb, unfortunately, is still not doing well and is now on dialysis, though they are still praying together. No matter the outcome of her illness, I believe those prayers will continue to sustain them, and we are grateful to know that our witness made a difference in their lives.

But the experience that really stands out in my mind when I think of our ministry during our cancer years involved another young man we met while in Seattle. Marshall and his wife, Heather, were also preparing for a bone marrow transplant at the Hutch, although his particular regimen would be a little different from mine. We met them one day in the hotel lobby and began talking together. And for some reason, as a form of encouragement for this young couple, Bob and I developed the habit of writing out little cards with verses from the psalms and slipping these under Marshall and Heather's door. We did this every day after our morning devotions.

We had been slipping cards under the door for a week or two when Heather asked if Bob would come over and pray with them while Marshall's mother was in town. Bob replied that it would be an honor. He even asked if we could bring Brad and Jenny and Bill, who happened to be visiting us. So the six of us had a sweet time together in Marshall and Heather's apartment. Bob read Scriptures, including John 3:16—a very important verse in this story. Then he anointed both Marshall and me with oil and we all prayed for healing.

The time for Marshall's bone marrow transplant came soon after that evening of prayer. The procedure went well, but then he developed an infection he just couldn't shake, and he was taken to the University of Washington hospital. He was not doing well at all. But he sent word to Bob that he had a story to tell.

By the time Bob and I were able to visit, the doctors were not holding out much hope for Marshall's recovery. He was already on life support when we saw him—with tubes and wires hooked up everywhere. The room was full of family and hospital staff, and there was no chance to talk privately. We just chatted briefly, prayed for Marshall, and went home.

At this point, Bob was really concerned about Marshall's salvation. That night he prayed, "Please give me one more day to talk to him."

The next day, when we went to visit Marshall again, only Heather and his parents were in the room. Heather and his father left for the airport to pick up his sister while

I took his mom into the hospital chapel to pray, leaving Bob alone with Marshall.

The end was clearly near. Marshall was gasping for breath. "I have to tell you...this story," he said. "When I was a little boy, I used to go to visit my uncle, and he made us memorize John 3:16. But all my life I never understood what it meant until that day in the hotel room when you anointed me with oil. Now I...I understand."

Bob was deeply moved. "Do you believe that God sent his Son? Do you understand about everlasting life through believing in Jesus our Savior?"

Marshall simply nodded yes. Then he added, "I'm so tired. I have to go to sleep."

"You just go to sleep," Bob told him. "Everything is going to be all right."

And it was. Marshall died that night, in his sleep. Bob and I were sad to lose our friend, sad to see such a young man succumb to such a terrible disease. But we also rejoiced to know that when Marshall died, he just slipped away into the arms of his heavenly Father. And what a joy to realize that God had used us, even in our time of deepest difficulty, to bring another lamb into his fold.

And that, of course, is the Lord's ultimate purpose in his call to us. It is the reason he became human in the first place, why he died for us, why he calls us to see and to help and to encourage and pray. Why he calls us to follow his example of sacrificial love and to extend that love in witness to others. Why he continues to live and work in cancer clinics and everywhere there is pain and loneliness and fear and sin and disbelief.

He does it because he loves us.

He does it because he has compassion on our pain and wants to rescue us from death.

He does it because he wants to use us in ministry—loving, being loved, and bearing witness—to reconcile the whole world to himself.

And he's doing just that—one hand, one heart at a time.

Dear Friend in Christ,

No matter what is going on in your life, there's no need to go through it alone. You're not *supposed* to go through it alone. You need other people, and they need you. God has made provisions, one way or another, for you to get the love and support you need—and you are part of God's provision for someone else.

If it doesn't *feel* that way, if you're feeling isolated and alone and purposeless, bring those feelings to the Lord. Lay your loneliness at his feet and ask him to help you. Ask him to show you ways to connect with others and share his blessings with them. Then try to be open to his answers. Remember, the Lord may not do things just the way you think he should, but he'll give you what you need for your journey.

Don't forget to ask for help if you need it—other people may not know. And don't forget to reach out. Pain or trauma can turn us inward and make us self-absorbed. But the simplest act of reaching outside yourself—even with just a smile or a hello—can help you make connections and start relationships.

The thing to remember is that God has a ministry for you, and you'll find it in the middle of your everyday life. There is an act of kindness, a word of encouragement, a gesture of love that only you can make.

Take a chance. Say yes. Open your heart and your hands. And be blessed.

From my heart to yours,

Emilie

—ᴄꜱ

GOD'S TRUTH FOR YOUR RELATIONSHIPS

ꜰ You were never intended to go through hard times alone.

ꜰ In the middle of your pain and difficulties, God is calling you to ministry—to be his hands and feet and ears and voice in a hurting world.

ꜰ Every moment of your life, in sickness and in health, you have the choice to withdraw into self or reach out to others.

ꜰ Your ultimate source for love and support is the Lord. But you can trust him to provide the human support you need.

ꜰ Your need can be a gift for someone who needs to reach out. Ask for it!

ꜰ Your deepest regrets will be those you could have helped. Even when you're hurting, reaching out to others will carry you toward peace.

ꜰ Your greatest gift of love toward another person is to share Christ with them.

—ᴄꜱ

CHAPTER EIGHT

What I Know That I Know

O LORD my God, I called to you for help and you healed me. O LORD, you brought me up from the grave; you spared me from going down into the pit.

—PSALM 30:2-3

For none of us lives to himself alone and none of us dies to himself alone. If we live, we live to the Lord; and if we die, we die to the Lord. So, whether we live or die, we belong to the Lord.

—ROMANS 14:7-8

I will sing to the LORD all my life; I will sing praise to my God as long as I live.

—PSALM 104:33

8

WHAT I KNOW
THAT I KNOW

Reflections on healing, death, and what comes next

⁘

I once watched an episode of *The Oprah Winfrey Show* in which Oprah asked her guests, "What do you know that you know? What is the bedrock of your belief system? What are you absolutely certain of?"

Well, that was an interesting, thought-provoking show. The answers Oprah received varied widely, although there were many common threads. And of course, that show also spurred Bob and me to ponder our own bedrock beliefs—to consider what it is that we absolutely know that we know.

When I ask myself that probing question in terms of my bout with cancer, a couple of things come to mind.

One thing I absolutely know is that God is good. That's our family's new motto. Jenny says it all the time, with childlike glee: "God is good, God is good, God is good."

We knew it before, but now we *really* know it—because his goodness has touched us in so many life-changing ways. Even when circumstances seemed unbearable, the Lord's goodness kept shining through. When we were all angry and confused about Jenny's divorce, he walked with us, gently guiding us toward the light, teaching us to trust and forgive and follow him. When cancer left us frightened, worried, and in various kinds of pain, we felt his embrace—both through loving human arms and his own comforting presence. When death loomed, he was still at work, crafting a bright future out of the darkest circumstances.

Throughout each ordeal, we felt the bedrock reality of God's goodness underneath us. And now we can look back from an easier perspective and see it with gorgeous clarity.

God is good. God is good. God is good. That's something I know that I know.

And here's another thing I know: God heals. I know this not just because I've read it in the Bible or met others who have been healed. I know it because he has worked a miracle of healing in my life. It came about a little differently than I expected—and it took a lot longer than I thought it would. But it was still a bona fide, praiseworthy, hallelujah-inspiring miracle. Actually, a series of miracles.

I recently looked back at some old journals and found this entry dated May 27, 1998: "This is the best day of my life because it's the beginning of my healing. I have a lot ahead of me, but I want to live to be a real wife to my Bob and Grammy to my grandchildren and a decent mom to Brad and Jenny. I know God is with me every step of the way and will hold me when I'm weak."

Looking back now, I realize I had no idea what actually lay ahead of me—hours and hours of chemo and radiation (plus bone marrow from an IV), bushels of hats and scarves, gallons of pills, two comas, three years of shingles agony, chubby cheeks, endless exhaustion, the works. And yet every single word I wrote in that long-ago journal entry turned out to be true. God did stay with me every step. God did hold me. And God did heal me—and not only of cancer.

Several years later, while I was in Seattle recovering from my bone marrow transplant, I was lying in bed. The discomfort from the shingles was very bad that morning. I tried to lie motionless, and still the burning, stabbing pain wrapped itself around my torso. TV was about the only pastime I could manage on mornings like that, so I turned on *The 700 Club*. During the "Word of Knowledge" segment, there was a mention of someone who had shingles. The host stopped and prayed that those shingles would be healed, and at that moment, something moved in my spirit. I sat up in bed, threw my hands in the air, and said, "I claim this healing!" I knew God was going to work in me and take away my shingles.

Bob came over and sat on the end of the bed and prayed with me that the shingles would be gone. But the pain was still there. And I kept asking, "When will it happen? When will I be cured?" Then Bob gently reminded me that I really didn't have shingles anymore. I had already been healed of the viral infection, and my ongoing pain was simply due to residual nerve damage. So we prayed that my damaged nerves would be healed and also that I would be given the grace to live with the pain.

Now, looking back, I realize that my spirit was right about that healing, too—though it took another couple of years. In the fall of that year, Dr. Barth sent me to a pain specialist, who for the first time was able to help me get just a little control over the pain. A year later, over the course of several months, I noticed the pain had diminished by almost half—most of the time. After that, month after month, the shingles pain was less of a problem. It's not gone. It may never be completely gone. But it's something I can live with—a significant and helpful healing.

God heals. I believe that with all my heart. And yet I have also come to believe that healing is a process we can't always understand. Even as I testify to my own physical healing, I can't forget the people I have met in the past four years who didn't make it. Many of these were Christians. Many were supported by prayer. Their doctors were just as skilled. And several even had more hopeful prognoses than I had. But I was healed, and they were not—at least, not on this side of paradise.

Healing is mysterious—and it's hard to avoid wondering why God heals one person and not another, or why he will heal one person spontaneously and heal another through a long process of medicine and prayer. I'm not sure I'll ever fully grasp the answers to those questions. But as I pondered the mysteries of healing, I've found it helpful to look at the gospels, to look at the way Jesus went about his ministry of healing and consider what that might tell me about the way God heals today.

Jesus, of course, was constantly surrounded by sick people during his earthly ministry—lepers, crippled people, blind people, people with blood disorders, the mentally ill. They approached him wherever he went, asking for a miracle. And he *always* said yes! He didn't tell them to suck it up and accept their fate and learn from their affliction. Instead, he responded in compassion and healed every single person who asked him to. I think that's important to recognize.

At the same time, Jesus rarely healed people the way others thought he should—and sometimes he didn't do it the way the sick people had in mind. Sometimes he did healing work on the Sabbath. Sometimes he laid hands on people, and sometimes he didn't even meet them face-to-face. Sometimes he used mud or saliva as healing tools. Sometimes he delayed when others thought he needed to act or acted when others thought he should lay low.

Jesus also infuriated the Pharisees by not limiting his ministry to physical healing. They were willing to let him cure blindness or leprosy if he could, but all that talk about forgiving sins crossed the line. But to Jesus, physical healing and spiritual healing were always part of the same package—and spiritual healing was his true focus. I think this is critical to note—Jesus was willing to perform "signs and wonders" but only to get people into the kingdom. He wasn't on earth just to heal bodies but to save souls and redeem lives.

And Jesus clearly didn't recognize death as a limit on his healing ministry. Realizing this has really helped me with my questions about who is healed and who isn't. Remember the story of Lazarus, when Jesus got word of his friend's illness but lingered where he was instead of rushing to the bedside? Lazarus, too, would eventually be healed, but he had to die first. And I've come to think that's true in our world as well. God heals, but healing is an ongoing process, and not every healing will be completed this side of death.

I'm not the first person to recognize that healing is not necessarily the same as a cure, but I think it's true. God's desire for us is total healing—for our bruised emotions, our traumatic memories, our troubled minds, our sin-sick souls as well as for our breakable bodies—as well as our ongoing growth and the furthering of his kingdom. He wants us strong, pure, unselfish, courageous, and kind, and he will do whatever is necessary to accomplish that goal. If curing our physical ills is the best way to help us move forward, he'll cure us. If our total healing is best served by letting us suffer a little while—or even by letting us die—he'll do that, too.

Through the years, some of God's most faithful servants have suffered from physical afflictions they carried with them to their deaths. I'm thinking of the apostle Paul, who claimed to suffer from a "thorn in the flesh" that God never healed. I'm thinking of Joni Eareckson Tada, who was paralyzed as a teenager and will most likely live out her life that way, but her radiant witness has never been confined to a wheelchair. I think of our friend Marshall, who came to know the Lord during his last days on earth. How they all must be rejoicing over the new, strong bodies they've been given (or in Joni's case, will be given) to match their beautiful, healthy spirits!

I have come to understand that God doesn't want any of us to be sick, although he is willing to *let* us be sick in order to accomplish other purposes. He has compassion on our pain. And when we come to him for help, he *will* heal us. But the way that healing is accomplished might be a surprise. It might not happen the way I thought or on the timetable I expected. It might not even be completed in my lifetime. God heals, but he will always do it his own way.

In my life, it happened through the skills of my doctors and nurses and through the power of prayer. But it did happen. Against all odds, there now is no sign of cancer in my body. My immune system is completely new. My shingles pain is subsiding. My hair is its normal length and color again. The chubbiness in my cheeks is almost gone.

Even better, I am more at peace now than I ever was. Repressed anger that used to masquerade as patience has dissolved into real patience. Resentments I struggled with for years are now far behind me. I am quicker to forgive, more willing to trust, more secure in my understanding that I am loved no matter what. My prayer life is deeper, my faith stronger. I'm far less driven and compulsive, and yet I am also bolder in my witness. I'm very aware that time is limited, and I don't want to waste any of it! My strongest priority in life is to tell people about the Lord who loves me, the Lord who saved me, the Lord who healed me. His love and health and salvation are available to them, too.

God has truly worked a miracle in my life. I am healed of my cancer. I am being healed of my shingles pain. I am growing toward complete healing of my body, mind, and spirit. And that brings me, oddly enough, to the third thing I'm absolutely certain about...which is that I am going to die!

I'm not trying to be flippant or morbid here. But one thing a bout with cancer will do in a person's life is bring her face-to-face with her own inevitable mortality.

The truth is, my cancer could come back at any time. Or I could be hit by a bus tomorrow. Or I could live to a ripe old age—which really isn't that far off—and then die quietly in my sleep. But death is going to happen to me. There's just no way around it.

Everyone who has ever lived on earth has died. (Well, maybe not Enoch or Elijah, but just about everyone else.) Even Jesus died, at least temporarily. Everyone Jesus knew in his lifetime, including the people he healed, eventually passed away. Every saint in every century has eventually gone to heaven. Every person who has been healed of disease or any other affliction will die.

And that's all right with me. It's more than all right. Because there's something else I know that I know that I absolutely know—which is that nothing can separate me from the love of Christ. Certainly not death.

I believe that the God who is in charge of all my days, who knows the beginning from the end, is absolutely loving and absolutely good. He is eternal, so he doesn't look at boundaries of life and death the same way I do. In my living and in my dying and then in my ongoing life with him, I know he will take care of me. Even better, he has a job for me.

I am well aware, you see, that the healing of my body is a wonderful, praiseworthy thing, but it's not the Lord's main concern. His goal is much bigger. In all our lives he is working to bring about his kingdom fully on earth, reconciling all creation—including me—to himself. Whether I die now or die later, I have the privilege of participating in that process, and that's perhaps the greatest gift I could ever receive.

A remarkable young man whom Bob and I have come to know—a 15-year-old cancer survivor—put the meaning of this gift so eloquently in a letter he wrote to me. It's a long letter, but I thought it was so beautiful I just had to share it with you:

> If I could tell you anything about cancer it is this…it has been the worst and most incredible thing that has ever happened to me. My name is Jonathan Baer, and I am a fifteen-year-old AML (acute mylogenic leukemia) cancer survivor. My story goes like this.
>
> It all started at my first high school track meet on St. Patrick's Day, 2001. That morning I woke up feeling the sickest I had ever felt. My mom thought I should push myself and go anyway, because I didn't tell her how sick I really was. So I ran, but my time was lousy. I felt awful afterward and started to cough up blood.
>
> That was the first physical symptom I had, and for the next two weeks I just got worse and worse. Because I was usually pretty healthy, nobody, including myself, was very concerned…

until my blood test results. The doctor told my mom to take me right to the emergency room because he was very concerned about my cell counts. When we got there, they took my blood again and told my family and me that I had leukemia....

I was told that my treatment would last six months, all in the hospital. They started me on chemotherapy the day after I was admitted. Then a few days later it started to hit me...and that's when I had an epiphany. God came to me one night while I was crying in my mom's arms. I kept saying, "This is too hard. I don't think I can do this." I had never felt so afraid in my life, so I just started to pray. I asked God right then and there how I was going to make it through this. Out of nowhere I said, "Trust in me...Mom, God just told me to trust in him."

From that moment on I knew if I trusted him through this, everything would turn out fantastic. I was hospitalized for the next four months. I suffered the worst pain I ever thought a person could take. The chemo, bone marrow, and spinal taps were routine. I lost 20 pounds and all of my hair. I had to face the fact that I might die. I saw other kids go through crazy things and didn't understand why.

Even though it was the hardest thing I had ever done, my situation seemed so much better than others. My doctors said I wouldn't be able to eat, I would spend a lot of time in the ICU for infections, and I wouldn't be able to go home during treatment. But I ate three meals a day, got only one infection, and was able to go home for short visits.

Before now it seemed like my belief in God was something I had done out of fear...kind of like "hell insurance." In the back of my mind I had always thought that there was a possibility God might not even exist. Sometimes when I would hear people speak at church about their experiences with God, I thought they believed in it so much that it just seemed real to them.

What happened to me with cancer totally changed my perception and my relationship with God. Now I know that God exists for sure, and no matter what, I cannot be convinced otherwise. God has shown me that the thing I feared most (death) can be as wonderful a gift as life is. If we didn't have death, life would not be as important or as enjoyable. I can really say that I am not afraid now. God has helped me countless times overcome all my fears and walked me through the hardest time of my life. God truly does work in mysterious ways. I know now that we can't take life for granted; we have to work hard and enjoy it as much as we can.

I feel like my life is the greatest gift that has ever been given to me. I'm living a dream that gets better every day. I love what I have and I love what has been given to me. That goes for all the mistakes I've made, and all the bad things that have happened to me, because if my life went any other way, it would not be as wonderful as it is right now.

What a blessing it is to realize that God is in charge of whatever happens, that he can make good use of whatever we have to endure—even death. That was true for Jonathan and for me, too. I believe it was a factor in my healing. I was able to trust him even when I was all but overcome with fear and worry and pain. Even when death seemed imminent.

I remember so clearly the trip to the airport to catch our plane to Seattle for my bone marrow transplant. Jenny and Bill drove us to the airport, and Jenny was crying hysterically the entire time. She wrapped her arms around me and would not let go. And I remember wondering why she was crying so hard. Then later, as I went through the preparations for the transplant and became aware of what would happen to me, I understood. Jenny was crying because she feared she'd never see me again. I was that close to dying, though I hadn't really grasped the fact.

Bob, too, was afraid that death might be the next step for me. At one point he even began to plan my funeral. He picked out songs and hymns ("How Great Thou Art," "Majesty," "My Tribute," "It Is Well with My Soul," "Amazing Grace") and did some thinking about what the service would be like and who would speak.

And I'll have to admit there were times during the course of my treatment, especially when the unrelenting pain from the shingles wore me down, that I wished the Lord would go ahead and take my life. When I would hear that someone I knew had died—especially a young person—I would wonder, "Why them and not me?" And I had plenty of moments when I just wanted it all to go away.

But at the same time, I found that the very possibility of my death awakened something surprising in me—an intense desire to live, a sense that I wasn't finished yet with what God wanted for me here on earth.

Before my cancer, I'll have to admit I was sometimes a little ambivalent about living. I wasn't suicidal! I liked my life fine. But I just wasn't that passionate about living. The idea of death seemed like a sweet, welcoming thing to me, an opportunity to rest and be with the Father.

Who knows why I felt that way? Maybe I was a little depressed…or just tired! But then I got sick, and something in me clicked into a different gear. I realized I wasn't ready to go yet. I needed to see my grandchildren grow up. I needed more time with my family. I needed more time to witness for my Lord.

On my birthday in 1999, I received a beautiful poster from my little grandson Bradley Joe. "I don't want Grammy to have another birthday," it read. "I don't want her to be old. I want to keep her forever." Well, I know he won't have me forever. But I believe that poster was a gift of God to remind me not to check out until it's time to go.

I remember an afternoon when I awoke from a nap to hear Brad and Bob talking in the other room. My sensitive, loving son was saying, "We want to do everything we can to make mom's last year with us the happiest and best it can possibly be."

Well, that moment *really* turned my spirit; it awakened the fighter in me. I thought, "Brad Barnes, I'm going to show you. I'm going to live *many* years." I really believe God used that little flare of indignation to stir me up a little, to enlist my fuller cooperation in the healing he was working in me, to show me he still had plans for me here on earth.

And so I didn't die. But I really am prepared to go—now or later. I think most believers feel that way, though we may dread the actual process of dying. In my case, I feel I've given the entire issue of dying over to God. And so far, his answer has been to keep me here. Through the entire ordeal of my cancer I have felt him gently guiding me and pulling me over one obstacle after another, from one step to the next, and so far the next step has not been death. Tomorrow it might be.

Either way, I'm all right, because of yet another thing I know that I know—which is that God can use everything that happens to me for his glory and his purposes.

I really mean *everything*. I'm talking about addictions and abuse. About family squabbles and estrangements among friends. About affairs and divorces. Bankruptcies and betrayals. Chronic illness and pain. Terrorist attacks.

Whatever awful things happen on this fallen planet, God can use it all for his glory. He can do amazing things with our most painful circumstances.

I think of a young man named Francis Chan, whom Chad met at a youth conference. Talk about a difficult set of circumstances—poor Francis' whole young life was a difficult circumstance! His mother died giving birth to him. His father raised him as a single parent until he was nine, then sent him to live with a beloved aunt and uncle—who were promptly killed in an auto accident. Francis went back to live with his father and stepmother, but his father died of cancer when Francis was in high school. Then Francis went to live with an uncle, who shot himself!

Despite all these painful losses, Francis managed to graduate from high school. He came to know Christ and went into ministry to teenagers. And believe me, they listen when he talks to them about what Jesus can do with our pain!

My grandson Chad certainly listened. Right now he's leading a group in his church for other young people who have been hurt by divorce. Like Francis, Chad is determined to let the Lord bring good out of his own troubles.

That's what I want to happen with my life, too—and I know it can. I know that I know that the Lord can take the pain of my cancer years and use it to advance his kingdom. Perhaps it will be through speaking and with interviews, perhaps through books, perhaps through something I haven't even thought of, like a little sharing group that meets in my home or a ministry of directed prayer for cancer patients or medical personnel. Whatever it is, I'm excited to realize that God will bring good out of what has happened me.

But there's a caveat, of course. God *can* do all those things with my pain and sorrow, but I have to let him. I don't get to direct the shots or do things my way. And yet I do have to participate. And I have to do the work. I have to obey him, to do what Scripture tells us and listen to those little urges telling us to do something we would never do otherwise. Sometimes I have to forgive when forgiving hurts my pride or give when I'd rather take. Sometimes I have to move when I'd rather stay put or stay put when every instinct tells me to move.

But I want to do that. I want to obey because, once again, the Lord is good. Because he has healed me. Because he uses everything that happens—even my death—for his glory. All these are things I know that I know.

What I don't know with any certainty is what will happen next in my life. I know I will rest and gain strength. I know I'll continue to have periodic checkups. But now that the cancer no longer dominates my days, I'm looking ahead and wondering what the Lord has in store for me.

I'm beginning to get a few inklings. I've done some interviews and tried out a few book ideas. I've begun accepting a few speaking engagements. At the same time, I'm determined to stay off the treadmill I was pounding so heavily before my cancer was diagnosed. I was doing God's work, but I now believe I was doing it too fast, too hard. I was never actually a workaholic—my home and my family were too important to me to neglect. But I neglected myself, neglected to pay real attention to my body's signals. And I was often so occupied with putting on the next seminar that it was hard for me to hear what God might have to say about slowing down and moving in a new direction.

Well, I've slowed down now!

In fact, I believe that getting me off the conveyer belt was one of God's gifts in my illness. For so long I just moved along, carried by our very efficient system, but without enough down time to really listen to God. Cancer gave both Bob and me the down time we needed. It also cleared our schedule and reduced our household responsibilities, freeing us to move in new directions. Most important, it reminded us of what matters most—our relationship to God, our relationship with each other and with our family and friends, our simple witness to the Lord's goodness.

We are realizing anew that ministry is not our first priority; obedience is. It's not up to us to take on the world, even for the Lord's sake. It's up to us to watch what he's doing and follow, to listen to his voice and follow. If we're doing that, we'll be successful, even if we never hold another seminar or write another book.

At the same time, I am very aware that time is short. I believe God has spared my life for a purpose, and I don't have that many more years on earth to fulfill that purpose. So I am eager to get going! I've been putting a few things on the calendar for next year, praying that God will show me what comes next. And the Lord has already given me a few new jobs—such as counseling with the parents of a friend of Brad's who has cancer. But I don't have any specific designs on the future at this point. I'm willing to trust God with that.

The Lord, after all, has given me more than I ever imagined. To have books in airports and speak on a platform before several thousand women who actually wanted to listen to me—that was a privilege I could never have dreamed of. It had to be God because I never could have dreamed it up on my own. And I believe that God, who is always good, still has work for me to do on behalf of his kingdom.

I'm willing if he is.

And that's something I know that I know that I know.

MY DEAR FRIEND,

If I could leave you with just one thought as we close this time together, it would be "Do it now!"

Whatever you've dreamed of doing in your life, whatever you have felt God calling you to do...go ahead now and take the first step. Whatever estranged relationship has haunted your heart...reach out now for reconciliation. Whatever "holy nudges" have urged you to call a friend or hug a grandchild—pay attention now.

Because time is short. I'm more aware of that now than I ever was.

My ministry is More Hours in My Day because it teaches skills that can help us make more of the time we're given. But the truth is that we really can't put more hours in our days or more days in our life.

God, who loves us, numbers our days—but we don't know how many we will have.

God, who loves us, will direct our paths—but we don't know where they will take us.

Any number of things could happen tomorrow. A cancer diagnosis. An accident. A financial reversal. Death. And though none of these disasters can separate you from Christ, they can still change everything about your life. They can rob you of precious time.

So live fully now. Take soup to your neighbors or point out the stars to your children now. Feed the hungry and visit the sick and share the Good News of Christ right now.

God has given you the gift of this moment, this day—and it's full of blessings and opportunities. But gifts were made to be used, not just stored on a shelf. So tear off the wrapping, pull apart the tissue paper, and say yes to what you find.

Most of all, say yes to the Lord who loves you. Give him back the gift of your hours and your days. Trust him to teach you, to care for you, to heal you, to help you grow.

Today, and tomorrow, you'll find he has wonderful things still up his sleeve.

Yours in Christ, today and tomorrow,

Emilie

⁓

GOD'S TRUTH FOR EVERY DAY
OF THE REST OF YOUR LIFE

♭ God is good. God is good. God is good.

♭ God heals—but he does it his own way. And he wants to heal the whole person, not just a disease.

♭ Death happens—but Christ is the Lord of death. So death is really just a change of address.

♭ Anything that ever happens to us can be a building block for God's kingdom.

♭ Every moment of our lives is an extravagant gift from the God who loves you! Don't forget to say thank you.

⁓

Every Day
Is Christmas

*Whom have I in heaven but you? And earth has nothing
I desire besides you. My flesh and my heart may fail, but
God is the strength of my heart and my portion forever.*

—PSALM 73:25-26

*All the days ordained for me were written in your book
before one of them came to be.*

—PSALM 139:16

EVERY DAY
IS CHRISTMAS

I've given a lot of Christmas gifts in my day.

Last year, however, was the first time I've ever *been* a Christmas gift!

It all started when Bob and I were out shopping. Just being out and about after years of confinement was such a treat for me. The streets downtown were transformed with glittering lights. The mall seemed like a wonderland of beautiful sights and sounds and smells—and I could even taste the hot cider we bought at a little kiosk. I felt like a kid again, excited and alive to everything around me.

Bob was happy, too, with a spring in his step I hadn't seen in years. "You know," he told me as we drove down the street, "you're the best Christmas present of all this year for our family. Last year, we didn't even know you would be here!"

That's what gave me the idea.

On Christmas Eve, as planned, we went over to Jenny's. We enjoyed dinner together—the whole clan gathered together. Everyone was excited about going in to open presents, but Jenny said the kitchen had to be clean first. So everybody set to work. Everybody but Bob and me, that is.

We sneaked out to the garage where I had stashed a bag of supplies. Out of that bag came a big roll of Christmas paper, which Bob used to wrap me head to toe with only my head sticking out. Then he picked up the big red bow that I had sewn onto a hair clip, and attached it on top. I only stumbled once or twice—though I giggled a lot—as Bob walked me into the living room and helped me lie down under the tree. Then I heard him go to the kitchen and announce that Santa had brought the most wonderful present.

Imagine the scene when my family rushed to the living room and found *me* under the tree! There was clapping and cheering and a lot of laughter. (I was laughing just as loudly for pure joy.) Then they unwrapped me, and we all sat down to enjoy the rest of that holy day.

That experience of being a gift under the tree has stuck with me as I've moved into the new year and the rest of my life. It brought home to me with special poignancy just how precious is the gift of my life. Precious to me. Precious to my family. Precious to God.

It's hard for me to think of my life now without imagining a big red bow on top. And remembering the fun of being joyously unwrapped.

And that's the way I imagine you, too. Your life is also precious—an irreplaceable, one-of-a-kind original from the Giver of all good gifts. But this is not the kind of gift to set aside to open later. And it's not a gift for you alone. It's for everyone—you are truly God's gift to the world! Every moment of your life is precious and important, to be received with gratitude and unwrapped with joy and then shared like a box of delicious chocolates.

And here's the interesting thing I've learned from 60-plus years of living, including four difficult years of cancer treatment. With the gift of life, the more you give away, the more you receive. Heaped up. Overflowing. With a big red bow on top.

Because "God so loved the world that he gave his one and only Son, that whoever believes in him shall not perish but have eternal life" (John 3:16).

Which means, of course, that for every one of us who chooses to receive that gift, every day of our life is going to be Christmas!

NOTES

1. Terry Healey, "At Face Value: My Struggle with a Disfiguring Cancer," on Steve Dunn's, CancerGuide website, http://www.cancerguide.org/thealey_story.html.

2. Larry Keefauver, *When God Doesn't Heal Now* (Nashville: Thomas Nelson, 2000), p. 69.

3. Cappy Capossela, quoted in E. Bingo Wyer, "That's What Friends Are For," *Good Housekeeping*, Dec. 1995, p. 30.

Other Harvest House Books
by Emilie Barnes

Abundance of the Heart

*Emilie's Creative
Home Organizer*

The Heart of Loveliness

Help Me Trust You, Lord

Fill My Cup, Lord

Survival for Busy Women

A Cup of Hope

More Hours in My Day

*Keep It Simple for
Busy Women*

Strength for Today, Bright Hope for Tomorrow

Safe in the Father's Hands

Other Good
Harvest House Reading

BEYOND BREAST CANCER
by *Alda Ellis*

Alda Ellis, creator of Alda's Forever bath and body products, lost her mother to breast cancer. Here, she shares the moving testimonies of 12 women whose lives have been touched by this devastating disease. Through these uplifting stories, survivors and caregivers will find that, no matter how difficult or painful the journey may be, in Christ they will find courage and strength.

PRAYERS IN THE STORM
by *Sandy Clough*

Artist and author Sandy Clough joins her tender art with Scriptures and prayers to embrace hurting people with the warmth of God's presence. This meaningful book is for anyone in need of comfort, consolation, and the promise of God's love in the midst of life's storms.

LETTER TO A GRIEVING HEART
by *Billy Sprague*

In this personal letter to those facing the loss of a loved one, Billy Sprague revisits his own landscape of mourning—the tragic death of his fiancee, the loss of his beloved grandmother, the departure of a dear friend. With sensitivity and understanding, he writes about the numbing reality of grief's shadowland and the sources of light and hope, the wise words, the acts of kindness, and the surprising revelations that eased him forward, back into the land of the living.

BENEATH HIS WINGS
by *Carolyn Shores-Wright*

Come discover a place of comfort and compassion, a shelter that offers security and a refuge that brings reassurance. Underneath the loving cover of God's protective wings, you'll experience the joyous peace that comes when you place your heart in the hands of the heavenly Father.

GOD CARES ABOUT YOU
by *Marie Shropshire*

Marie Shropshire affirms God's ability to provide love and strength in any situation—be it grief, trouble, or the simple desire to rely more fully on the Lord.